MIRACLES
from the
ALASKA HIGHWAY

BRUCE GRANGER

The Alaska Highway

Dawson Creek, BC. Start of the Alaska Highway

Table of Contents

print ISBN: 979-8-35095-203-2
ebook ISBN: 979-8-35095-204-9

Bruce Granger Biography

Bruce at top of Atigun Pass, Dalton Highway, AK

Bruce Granger is a multi-faceted man with many interests. Most of his professional career has been in industrial real estate in Chicago. Prior to that career, he was the general manager of a distribution company, a college professor (Ph.D. in Sociology), a professional musician, and a truck driver/mover. He grew up on a farm in Ohio and credits much of his success to the values learned from the farm. His hobbies include aviation (private pilot), travel, and motorcycle adventure riding. His motorcycle adventures have taken him all over the North American continent from Labrador to Alaska. He is also a writer and has written three religious devotional books.

Introduction:

The Story

Fairbanks, Alaska
Saturday, June 17, 2023

Bruce standing in the mostly frozen Arctic Ocean

Two Suzuki Vstrom-1000 loaded and ready to depart for the Dempster Highway

Bryan Barus and Bruce Granger at Fairbanks, AK Airport

Valley and Mountains of Muncho Lake Provincial Park, Canada

The Alaska sun was already high in the sky by 8:00 a.m. The air had a nip in it as my riding partner, Bryan Barus, and I loaded our decked-out adventure, touring motorcycles for the big ride. Both bikes are Suzuki V-Strom 1000 machines, big enough to carry lots of gear over highways as well as gravel roads.

The excitement was building to leave Fairbanks and ride the Dempster Highway up to the Arctic Ocean. The Dempster is a 1,200-mile gravel road full of potholes, switchbacks, wildlife, and incredible scenery.

This was Bryan's first time riding in Alaska and Canada. Two other previous experiences in Alaska for me only made me hungry to hit the open road again. Riding in Alaska and northern Canada is filled with majestic views, lots of mountains, lakes that are crystal clear, bears, moose, and unlimited vistas. Riding a motorcycle brings the excitement of mastering a big riding machine while simultaneously enjoying the views. There are always challenges for which you need to be prepared, like changing weather and road conditions.

This morning, the bright sun was warming the chill of the air. Yes, it was still cool enough to wear a down-filled jacket under the Klim riding gear to stay warm.

We head east, out of Fairbanks, for the couple-hour ride on the paved Alaska Highway. We headed to Tok, Alaska, to pick up the gravel on the Dempster Highway. I let Bryan lead the way so that he could experience every Alaska riding experience for the first time.

Picture of Dalton Highway similar to Dempster Highway.

As we rode through the town, North Pole, we were on the lookout for Santa, but he must have been sleeping. As we pass a golf course, the sign says, "Special on 10:30 p.m. tee off times!" What is not to enjoy about the almost twenty-four-hour sunlight in this part of the world in summer?

The morning sun is bright and warming as the air comes over the windshield. The throttling sound of the two Suzuki V-Stroms screams plenty of power for the ride. The gear we are wearing is top-notch and ready for any kind of weather.

Eventually, we leave the metropolitan area and pass the Eielson Air Base on our way east out of town. The green grass from the long hours of sunlight colors the ditches as we eventually find ourselves in more remote areas. Often, there are areas of the Alaska Hwy, where you can ride for miles and not see anyone.

The Alaska Hwy stretches 1,500 miles from Dawson Creek, Canada, to Fairbanks, Alaska. The road was built during World War II in less than nine months as a necessary transportation road to defend Alaska. It is also referred to as the "Alcan," symbolizing the joint efforts of the US and Canada to build the road.

The Alaska Highway between Fairbanks and Tok weaves its way among a combination of flat land and gentle rising and falling terrain. With Bryan setting the pace, we were enjoying the scenery and beauty of riding in the Alaska open country.

We came around a gentle curve in the road with a turn-out section to the left. As the leader, Bryan decided to make a turn into the scenic turnout. I was riding in trail, standing on the pegs, cruise control on, and enjoying the ride.

To make the turn off behind Bryan, I needed to stop quickly. A quick squeeze on the front brake was made to turn off the cruise control . . . except it didn't. For some reason, it hung up ever so slightly and didn't disengage. But then it was released. By that time, there was too much brake squeeze on the front of the bike. The front brake locked up. From my standing position, I became a human missile flying over the handlebars at 65 mph.

As I flew through the air, time seemed to slow down. Several immediate thoughts passed through my head.

"I sure wish I had bought that Klim air-bag vest because this is going to hurt!"

And then a more ominous thought, *Is this the end?. Will I survive?!*

In the ensuing ten to twelve seconds, my body tumbled and rolled violently in an uncontrolled manner. My head and left shoulder took the initial hit. The rough asphalt carved deep gouges in the left side of my helmet. Since wearing top-of-the line riding gear is part of my standards, I knew I was not going to leave any skin on the road.

I continued to tumble, my arms and legs flailing like rag dolls. With each twist and turn, I could feel the pain increasing. *When is this ever going to stop?*

Eventually, skidding over the rough road brought me to a halt. I found myself lying on my back in the middle of the Alaska Highway, with the most excruciating pain I have ever experienced welling up inside me. Everything hurt. My head was throbbing inside my Shoei helmet. I tried to stand up, but quickly laid back down from the crushing pain and a broken ankle.

How is it that one minute I am healthy and excited to be doing something I love, and in a matter of seconds, life has changed?

My body is racked with pain, and life feels like it is hanging in the balance. Your mind is preoccupied with the pain. But it still has awareness of an alarming question. "Am I going to survive? What is life going to look like after this?" All these feelings and emotions are wrapped in physical pain and agony, and I am on the verge of losing consciousness.

It is easy to question God during a tragedy and ask, "Why? Why me?!" Where is God when you need Him? The answer to some of these questions came in very short order.

Bryan got to me and took a quick assessment. I was still conscious but groaning in deep pain. Lying in the middle of the road with sweeping curves in both directions meant that it was easy to get run over. Bryan made an immediate effort to stop any traffic from both directions.

The first car coming from the south stopped within about thirty seconds of my coming to rest in the middle of the highway. Out walked a man, identifying himself as a paramedic!!

Within another thirty seconds, the first car coming from the north stops. Two men jump out and rush to me, identifying themselves as airborne paramedic troupers!

Within one minute, God had provided the necessary resources to start the recovery process.

Isn't it interesting that God provided this coordinated effort in advance? The paramedics left their previous departure points and arrived from opposite directions at just the right time to be there for me. Only God can coordinate a miracle such as this.

The presence of these paramedics was like having multiple angels watching over me. They knew exactly how to access my physical condition. They were talking to me, engaging me in conversation to keep me conscious. They cut my coats off to access the damage underneath. It became comical when they started cutting my down jacket. The feathers were flying, and I could tell that was the last thing they wanted to see!

The skills of paramedics and medical professionals trained for these emergency situations are amazing. One of the paramedics was doing a physical assessment of me while the other was making notes. The paramedic reached under my jacket to feel my left side. I heard him say, "Looks like he has about nine broken ribs." Later x-rays would show that there were, in fact, nine broken ribs on the left side. These paramedics were angels in disguise.

The call was made for an ambulance from a rural fire department about forty-five minutes away. The paramedics were trying to keep me calm during the trauma. I was slipping into shock.

Eventually, the ambulance arrived. Oh no . . . more pain as they loaded me on a board to get me in the ambulance. I heard the counting from the medical people. The 1, 2, 3 signaled the coordinated count as they picked me up and shoved the board under me. My cries of pain were wrapped into the conversations of the medics doing their jobs.

The jarring gurney ride was made to the ambulance, and the jostling of the legs on the gurney, collapsing as they pushed me in the ambulance, only added to the already excruciating pain. With the ambulance still parked, the medics immediately began the process of trying to get a needle in my arm to deal with shock and get me stable. They were trying valiantly to find a vein, but they could not find it. I later laughed that it was a search for a vein in vain.

Time was marching on as the two medics in the back were working feverishly. The medic behind the wheel was also part of the conversations to get the IV started. Eventually, the driver said, "Time is wasting; we need to get rolling and headed to the hospital."

I remember the sinking feeling of not having the IV to help with the pain. The bouncing ambulance jostling over the road just made it that much worse. I thought they are never going to find a vein with this much bouncing. A short time later, I heard one of the medics say, "I got it!" I was so relieved. The drugs must have worked because I don't remember a lot of the hour and half ride to the Fairbanks Hospital. I must have been coherent enough, because I did remember the jostling on the gurney as they wheeled me into the hospital.

The emergency room doctors and crew did an amazing job. But there's not much I remember about the experience. Hours later, after many tests, probes, scans, and exams, I was taken to a hospital room. The night was a blur. Thank goodness for pain meds.

Fairbanks Memorial Hospital
Sunday, June 18

On Sunday and most of Monday, I was almost coherent. My mid-section was wrapped in tight bandages to stabilize the ribs. Meds kept the pain under control but made me loopy.

The doctor's initial assessment was that I was badly banged up with lots of broken bones. Nine ribs, my shoulder blade (scapula), and collarbone (clavicle) were all broken. (They would later find a broken ankle as well.) But so far, they could find no evidence of any significant internal injuries.

The helmet saved my life. The safety gear saved my skin from being ripped from my body.

Despite being sore and in pain, I was able to sit up for an hour or so on Sunday. In the afternoon, we set up a conference call, and I spoke by phone to my family. It seemed like I was going to be okay. There was no paralysis, and no apparent internal injuries.

Whew . . . I had dodged a bullet.

Fairbanks Memorial Hospital
Monday Afternoon, June 19

And then, Monday afternoon . . . wham. Things changed quickly. The lights went out.

My organs began to shut down. Vital signs were dropping. Alarms were ringing from the machines hooked for monitoring. Without delay, they rushed me into emergency surgery.

It was discovered that my colon had a tear. Waste was leaking into my body, causing infection. Sepsis developed and was ravaging my body. My life was now in grave danger.

Adventure Motorcycle Riding

What is it about being a motorcycle adventurer that motivates a rider like me? There are many factors which create this drive and motivation to go explore various parts of the world. Why not do it on a motorcycle?!

If you have ever ridden a horse, there is this sense of strength and power of the horse as it leaves the canter to a full gallop. You feel the powerful flanks of the horse moving in coordination and the fun of speeding across the ground on the powerful animal.

A motorcycle provides a similar feel. There is the thrill of feeling the power of the bike accelerate underneath you as you twist the throttle down and clutch through the advancing gears. There is the freedom of feeling the wind in your face as speed increases. There are all the various senses that are activated as you smell and observe the surroundings.

Yes, if you are a farm boy you can tell what kind of livestock is in a barn just by the wafting aroma that hits your nose at 60 mph. Fortunately give it thirty seconds, and it will be gone.

The greatest joy of riding a motorcycle is being outside and experiencing the beauty of the scenery around you as well as weather. Seeing the expanse of the mountains and the curvy roads that go with it engages the rider to experience those elements in a personal-touch manner.

All of the above are only part of the thrill of being on a motorcycle to experience life to the fullest. The challenges of riding, the beauty of seeing new things, the mastery of controlling a motorcycle in challenging conditions, and seeing new things, are all part of the allure and beauty of riding a motorcycle. These are the reasons I find myself in places like Alaska.

Fairbanks Memorial Hospital
Surgery Suite
Monday Evening, June 19

I was rushed into emergency surgery in Fairbanks to address the ruptured colon. Surgeons explored my insides to find the source of the leak. They discovered a sepsis infection had set in and was spreading. They acted quick to stabilize the infection, remove the contaminated parts, and keep me alive.

Sepsis is a serious condition in which, the body responds improperly to an infection. The infection-fighting processes turn on the body, causing the organs to work poorly or shut down completely. There is a dramatic drop in blood pressure that can cause the lungs, kidneys, liver, heart, and other organs to be damaged. When left unchecked, sepsis becomes severe, and can lead to death.

The sepsis was advancing quickly. In fact, they said it progressed to the third stage of sepsis called septic shock. And that's very bad.

Their expertise was my lifeline. A tear was found in my colon caused by the trauma of the fall and tumble. A four-foot section of my colon was removed. Scar tissue and infected parts were cut away. My innards were packed with meds to kill the infection.

But now, I had a problem. With the section of colon removed, there was no way of discharging waste. They stapled off the rest of my colon and installed an ostomy bag on my side.

Over the next twenty-four hours, my condition did not improve. The doctors pushed me into a medically induced coma. I have no recollection of anything that happened over the next seven to eight days.

By Tuesday afternoon, the severity of the sepsis led the medical staff to recommend relocating me to Anchorage. The hospital there had greater capacity to deal with the life-threatening situations.

This was the period my family was notified and told things were very serious, and life was hanging in the balance.

Late in the afternoon on Tuesday, I was wheeled out of Memorial Hospital and loaded onto a Med Flight Learjet for the flight to Anchorage. With the concern about my life, my family was able to follow the flight through FlightAware, a software program that tracks aircraft flights.

Anchorage, Alaska
Providence Medical Center
Wednesday, June 21

Providence Hospital in Anchorage is a world-class hospital. It is large enough to handle challenging cases. Over the course of the next several days, they performed three additional surgeries in my abdomen to address the sepsis. An additional operation was performed to remove fluid from the left lung, and yet another surgery was performed to repair my broken shoulder with metal plates and screws. They went into my chest so many times, they didn't even bother sewing the incision back up.

I have absolutely no recollection of those days.

Providence Medical Center
Wednesday, June 28

After eight days, the effects of the coma wore off, and I awoke to lots of confusion. My body was racked with lots of pain from the accident and six surgeries. Any movement meant pain. I found myself lying on my back in bed with hoses hooked up to every orifice I had, along with electrodes tracking my every heartbeat.

Because of the eleven-inch open wound in my abdomen, which needed to heal from the inside out, they placed a wound-vac on me. The purpose of the wound-vac is to pump good fluid through the wound and remove infection. I would ultimately have this unit on for close to seventy days while at the hospital.

Life in the hospital would begin to take on a routine with regular blood draws, a change of the wound-vac every three days, daily pills to swallow, feeding through a nose tube, antibiotics fed through an IV, doctors' visits, and eventually movement out of bed. Since I was immobile, a Hoyer lift was used to lift me out of bed into a wheelchair. That meant that I could be wheeled around and even outside for some fresh air.

During my stay, the medical professionals worked on several problems. They continued to address the sepsis and got it under control. My limbs needed physical therapy to regain movement. They worked me over well. My voice was so weak. They sent in specialists to help me regain speech, swallow, and other simple tasks.

Each day brought small but incremental gains. I was making progress. My stay at Providence Hospital started in the ICU. After some progress, I moved to Acute Care. More progress meant I could move into a regular hospital room.

The seventy-two days I spent in the Alaska hospitals seemed to fly by quickly. Each day brought a new challenge or new task, which was addressed. I was exceptionally blessed by family members plus three special friends who each came and spent time with me in the hospital for the entire seventy-two days.

Having family and friends present to advocate on my behalf was so beneficial to my recovery. Often, they would see things that needed to be addressed and make sure they were given full detail. The nurses and doctors were always amazed when there would be a "changing of the guard" and a new family member or friend would show up. They would make comments like: "You are so lucky to have such special support." They were absolutely right; I was especially blessed by their presence.

It is humbling when you realize you have to relearn the muscle memory for basic life skills. One of the first skills to relearn was swallowing. Because of concerns about fluid getting into my lungs and me aspirating, it took a series of lessons and experiments to figure out how to swallow properly. Eventually, they sat me up in bed to learn balance. The first time the nurse set me up in bed, she turned away for a second, and it resulted in me falling back into the bed as the equilibrium wasn't quite there. Simple tasks like being able to get myself out of bed and into a sitting position were excruciating with pain and effort.

Anchorage, Alaska
St. Elias Specialty Hospital
July, 10

The doctors determined that I was ready to begin a more intensive rehabilitation. They moved me to St. Elias Specialty Hospital, a couple of blocks from the main Providence Medical Center. The program called for five to seven hours per day of intense physical therapy.

It was hard to imagine how I was ever going to be able to do this, given that I could barely set up in bed. The daily therapies, both physical and occupational, required lots of effort and were tremendously draining physically. There were times where I would have a forty-minute break between sessions, and I would beg to be put back in bed so I could rest/sleep for any minutes I could get.

Due to the lengthy time in a hospital bed, I had to re-learn the muscle memory to walk again, climb stairs, develop dexterity in my left hand that had some nerve damage, strengthen my shoulders, button my shirt, and even learn how to cook my own grilled cheese sandwich.

The day came when the insurance company and the doctors determined I was stable enough to travel. There were personal questions as to whether I was strong enough physically to make the trip, but plans were made, and I felt like the bird getting kicked out of the nest. There clearly were apprehensions on my part and others about making the trip. The travails with the ostomy bag made life exceptionally challenging, with great effort to keep it attached to me.

American Airlines Flight 1233
Anchorage to Dallas-Fort Worth
Monday, August 28

The day came to fly to Dallas, TX, where my rehabilitation was to continue. The eight-hour flight required me to leave the hospital at 4:00 a.m. to get to the airport. At 3:30 a.m., the nurses at the hospital were still wrestling with keeping the ostomy bag attached to me. How was I ever going to make it to eight hours without it coming off? Changing an ostomy bag is challenging. I knew I could do it, but it would be difficult given my other physical limitations.

Having someone fly with me was a real godsend. My brother-in-law, Gerald Oliver, came to Alaska to make the trip back to Dallas. His organization and attention to detail got us to the airport, navigated my wheelchair through the terminal, got me situated on the airplane, and out of the Dallas airport to the rehabilitation facility. To say I am blessed by a wonderful family would be an understatement.

The location of Dallas was chosen for rehabilitation because there was a room available at a rehab/assisted living facility. My sister and brother-in-law, Kathy and Gerald Oliver, would be close to assist.

The next four months involved continuing physical therapy to get stronger and nursing care to aid in the healing of the open wound, which was still present when I left Alaska.

A key component of the recovery process was mentally getting back into doing computer work so I could continue my business of industrial real estate in Chicago. Initially, my capacity to sit and work on the computer was less than an hour before there would be headaches. Just as I was building physical strength by walking, I was also having to stretch my mind and time at the computer as well.

Midlothian, TX
Midlothian Methodist Hospital
Tuesday, December 12

The last major piece of the recovery process was having surgery to reverse the ostomy bag, which could not be done for at least six months. To accomplish this procedure and to reconnect my internal plumbing, the original eleven-inch incision in my abdomen was reopened.

Although it had taken seven months for the original incision to heal, it was necessary to reopen it to complete the reversal surgery. The recovery from the surgery was challenging, but eventually, after several months, the wound healed, and the physical therapy was completed.

Miracles Happen

When the tragedies of life happen, one is faced with challenges that stretch the physical, mental, emotional, and spiritual sides of life. The fact that I survived a horrific motorcycle accident gave way to an appreciation of the many miracles that took place as a part of the accident and recovery process. The many miracles are directly related to God's intervention in so many ways.

As a minister prayed for me in the hospital, he said the following: "God's mercies and grace are for the impossible." Clearly, God's hand was present to allow my survival and ability to become a walking miracle.

God's mercy and grace are for the impossible! During the course of my Alaska journey, there were many dark moments. There were moments where pain, suffering, confusion, uncertainty, fear, questions of why, and questions of the future were forefront in my mind.

What was the purpose of all these experiences? Why was I able to survive when someone else may have lost their life? Considering the odds of my accident and the subsequent medical issues that could have easily taken my life, why was I able to survive?

When I ask these questions, I can only come to rest in the truth of the chaplain's comment. God's grace and mercy are for the impossible. What an amazing medical and personal journey it has been.

The real story for me has been the many miracles that happened along the journey that have been such a part of my recovery. Many of these miracles are clearly the result of God watching out for me and providing His angels to watch over me. This book is an attempt to tell those stories.

I believe in the power of prayer. The prayers of many people on my behalf were instrumental in God enabling the healing process to take place like it did. I am so grateful to God, my family, special friends, and many doctors, nurses, and therapists, who were so instrumental in nursing me back to health.

My hope is that the stories from these experiences will be an inspiration to others who may be going through similar personal challenges in their lives. God's promise to be with us is the truth! Whatever the outcomes may be from a tragedy, God still provides His presence and will.

I love adventure and riding motorcycles. Do I believe God uses all things for our good? Yes! Do I wish to go flying over the handlebars again? No! But if my experiences can encourage someone and give hope, I'm glad I have been able to share my journey with you.

Miracle 1:

Accident Location

Alaska Highway

Alaska is the largest state in the United States. It is also one of the least populated states, with fewer roads and more remote locations. The intent of the motorcycle trip was to go from Fairbanks, AK, up the Dempster Highway, through the Northwest Territory, and past the arctic circle to touch the Arctic Ocean at Tuktoyaktuk, Canada.

The Dempster Highway is a gravel road that crosses the Peel and Mackenzie Rivers via ferries, goes over North Fork Pass Summit, and has lots of tundra. The remoteness of the highway means services are limited and access to fuel must be planned.

The location of where an accident takes place is a big factor in how quickly, if at all, emergency services can be accessed. Most of the 1200-mile round trip to the Arctic Ocean is a gravel/dirt road, with only a few small towns sprinkled along the way. If the accident had happened along the remote Dempster Highway, getting services would have taken a significant amount of time and expense.

The departure from Fairbanks to the town of Tok, Alaska, meant a several-hour ride down the paved Alaska Hwy before getting to the graveled Dempster Highway. If an accident is going to happen, being on the main Alaska Highway, as remote as it is in sections, provides the best opportunity for emergency services.

My travel partner, Bryan Barus, and I were about an hour and a half out of Fairbanks on the Alaska Highway when the accident occurred. Even with the distance of an hour and a half to Fairbanks via an ambulance ride, it was much quicker and more fortunate for me to get to medical facilities than being on the remoteness of Dempster Highway.

It is a miracle that the accident allowed several things to occur. As a part of God's plan, I was fortunate to have three paramedics arrive at the accident scene within one minute of me rolling to a stop. The chances of this happening along the Dempster Highway would have been unlikely, as the road is less traveled. The accident location allowed the response of a local rural fire department to get to me with an ambulance and transport me to Fairbanks.

Should the accident have taken place further up the Dempster Highway, the distance from the medical facility would have been much greater. The logistics of getting from the accident scene to Fairbanks would have likely required a significant effort, either via timing for an ambulance to travel up the Dempster or employing the services of a medical helicopter. In either case, the timing of getting to medical services would have been significantly longer.

I am so grateful that the location of the accident allowed access to medical transport and services within a reasonable time period. God was clearly watching out for me.

Miracle 2:

Out-of-Control Motorcycle

Bruce's Shoei Helmet meets the asphalt of the Alaska Highway

A common practice on an adventure touring bike is to stand on the pegs to stretch the legs and back. The standing felt good, and the scenery around me was spectacular. As I was trailing my riding partner, he decided to make a quick turn into a turnout area to take in the scenery. My cruise control was on, and I needed to quickly turn it off.

Turning the cruise control off is much like in a car. You can tap the brake, and it will turn off. I had chosen to tap the right front brake handle to turn the cruise control off. Unfortunately, the untimely release of the cruise control and the simultaneous locking of the front brake were not a good combination. The combination of these two events sent me flying over the handlebars at 65 miles per hour.

With the front brake locked up, I was catapulted off the front of the bike and sent violently tumbling and rolling down the road. As I was going over the handlebars, my first thought was, *I sure wish I had bought that Klim airbag vest . . .because this is going to hurt!* The second thought was, *Is this the end?!*

I believe in wearing all the gear all the time. I knew I was not going to leave any skin on the road, but I knew my body was going to take a beating. The tumbling and turning felt like every part of my body was going in different directions, and I could feel added pain with every bounce and turn.

Eventually, I came to a stop in the middle of the Alaska Highway, lying on my back in excruciating pain and agony.

Also tumbling and rolling down the road was the Suzuki Vstrom 1000 motorcycle. This is a large adventure touring bike, which, when fully loaded, weighs about 720 lbs. While I was being catapulted down the road, simultaneously, the heavy bike was also on a path of its own without a rider. It was not until months later that I was studying some pictures taken of me lying in the middle of the road that I realized the skid marks of the motorcycle were about six inches from my head.

While I was grateful to be wearing one of the best and most expensive helmets available, it is hard to say what a 720 lb. weight would have done to my head, or any other part of my body should it have run over me as part of its path to stopping.

It gives me chills when I think how miraculous it was that God used His angels to protect me from further injury or even a fatal impact with the out-of-control motorcycle. I know God had His hand in that series of events, protecting me. Thank you, God.

Miracle 3:

Paramedics Arrive

First Paramedic on scene with Bruce laying on Alaska Highway

Paramedics and Bruce on Curve of the Alaska Highway

Airborne Paramedic Troupers doing a Physical Assessment of Bruce

Alaska Highway blocked for Protection of Bruce in Road

Bruce laying on Alaska Highway waiting on Ambulance.

Paramedics keeping Bruce calm until the ambulance arrives. Notice close proximity of motorcycle tire skid marks to Bruce.

After the violent thrashing of my body, twisting, turning, and tumbling down the road, I came to a stop in agony and pain. While I was still conscious, the level of pain was excruciating. My fellow motorcycle partner, Bryan Barus, quickly got to me. Unfortunately, where the accident happened was somewhat obscured by a slight curve in the road. He was concerned about getting cars stopped so as not to hit me since I was lying in the middle of the Alaska Hwy.

However, within thirty seconds of my coming to a halt, the first car coming from the south stopped. The driver walked up and identified himself as a paramedic. He immediately started to access my needs. Within thirty seconds after the paramedic got to me, the first car from the north stopped and up walked two airborne paramedic troopers. They jumped in and added their trauma expertise, which included accessing bodily damage and mobilizing transport services.

The two airborne troupers were experts at accessing trauma situations. One of them was taking notes as the other trouper was accessing my physical situation. They cut my coat to see if there was any bleeding. The trouper doing the accessing reached in on my left side and felt my ribs. He casually said to the other paramedic trouper taking notes, "Yep, looks like he has nine broken ribs!" It was ironic that later, when the hospital staff took full x-rays, they concluded there were nine broken ribs!

How can I not praise God for providing that level of expertise in such a short time? These men were clearly God's angels, placed there at the accident scene to provide care. Their presence and demeanor kept me calm and prevented me from going into shock. I only wish I knew their names to thank them.

I recognize that God promises to be with us in good and bad times. This particular day, in the midst of a bad circumstance, He provided a level of unbelievable medical help that only God could orchestrate. How miraculous it was that paramedics coming from opposite directions would converge on my accident scene to provide the immediate medical attention provided within one minute of time.

Some might call this luck. I call it God-inspired actions. God is willing to use others for His purpose and to be His angels.

Thank you, God, for the gift of these three wonderful angels who were used to help save my life.

Miracle 4:

People helping people.

Damaged Bike at good Samaritan's House

Bruce's damaged bike loaded in trailer for trip back to Chicago.

Approximately forty-five minutes after the accident, an ambulance arrived and transported me to Fairbanks Hospital. My travel partner, Bryan Barus, was left at the accident scene, trying to sort through the options of what to do with my broken motorcycle, called "Crazy," that was lying along the side of the road. While talking with the police officer on site and others, he was trying to determine the best plan of action.

To show that God has a sense of humor, there was a couple headed to their home in Fairbanks with an empty trailer. They approached Bryan and offered to transport the crippled bike to Fairbanks, where Bryan could later retrieve it and load it into my trailer to transport back to Chicago. They said, "We know you don't know us, but we are also motorcyclists and would welcome the opportunity to help by taking the bike to Fairbanks for you. We had gone to pick up another bike, but it wasn't ready, so we have an empty trailer!"

Again, two kind angels stepped up and helped in what was a very stressful situation.

A day or so later, when Bryan went to the couple's home to retrieve the bike, he said they were the nicest and kindest people you would want to meet. Later in my recovery, when I was able, I sent them a thank-you card. When I go back to Alaska, I will reach out to these fine people and thank them for their act of kindness.

God's angels were at work,, even in the smallest of details.

Miracle 5:

All the Medical Angels

Paramedics and Ambulance Crew Making plans for Transport.

Paramedics and Ambulance crew loading Bruce on Stretcher

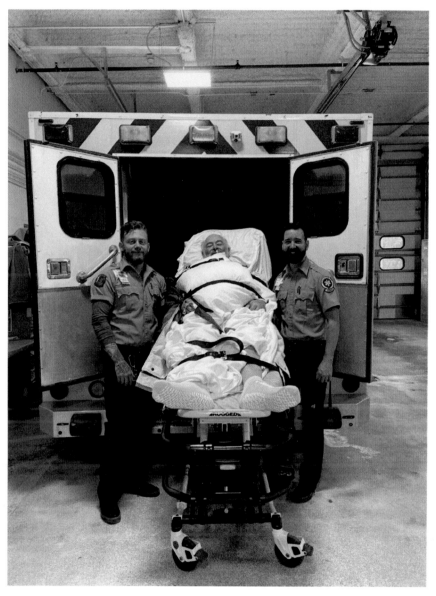

Paramedics Transporting Bruce between Providence Hospital and St. Elias Specialty Hospital. Shortly after transporting Bruce, they went and got him an iced Starbucks coffee!

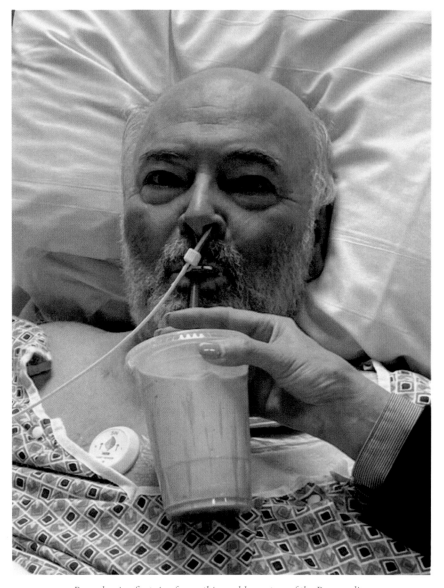

Bruce having first sip of something cold courtesy of the Paramedics.

Throughout the initial part of the accident, the subsequent surgeries, and the lengthy rehabilitation, I was blessed with so many good medical people who assisted in my recovery. Thank you, God, for all the paramedics, nurses, doctors, pilots, and ambulance drivers who saved my life. So many "angels" who stepped into the gap to save my life. Thank you, Jesus.

When I think about all the medical people involved in my accident recovery and subsequent hospital experiences, I am amazed at the number of people and medical disciplines involved. Below is a list of incredible people who were special to me:

1. Paramedics at the accident scene.

2. Ambulance paramedics.

3. Fairbanks Emergency Room Doctors and Nurses.

4. Fairbanks doctors and nurses who performed surgery on me.

5. Pilots and medics for the life-flight from Fairbanks to Anchorage.

6. Providence Hospital doctors, nurses, and specialists who performed multiple surgeries.

7. St. Elias Specialty Hospital doctors and nurses.

8. A multitude of physical and occupational therapists at St. Elias.

9. Specialty wound doctors and nurses who also worked with the ostomy bag and maintenance.

10. Surgeons in Texas to reverse the ostomy bag.

11. Kidney doctors.

12. Personal care physician.

All of these people provided unbelievable knowledge and efforts to help repair my broken body. Their medical gifts were priceless! All of these medical people were angels in disguise.

At one point, the doctors at Providence released me to be transported to the St. Elias Specialty Hospital. The transport team of paramedics came with their stretcher to provide the necessary transport. I remember the kindness and gentleness of the two young men as they moved me from bed to stretcher and stretcher back to a bed in the new hospital. They were young, energetic, engaging and kind in their dealing with my pain as they made the transitions. They loaded me in their ambulance. My sister Kathy Oliver was with me riding along taking her first ride in an ambulance. She was chatting in a friendly manner with the young men telling a little of my story/accident. I could barely talk since my voice had been softened by weeks of a tube in my throat. As part of the conversation she mentioned I was looking forward to eventually having something cold to drink, since up to that point I had only been allowed ice chips.

The surroundings of the new hospital were distanced in my mind as I delt with pain while being transferred from the gurney of the paramedics to the new bed. The young guys smiled, apologized for causing the pain and graciously left.

New doctors and nurses were coming and going to get me checked into the St. Elias Specialty Hospital. The room had been a buzz of activity. About a half hour after arriving, who should come walking through the door, again, but these two young paramedics. Their presence caught me by surprise until I looked at one of them and he was carrying an ice-cold Starbucks coffee. I started to cry at the kindness shown by these fine young men who went the extra mile to show compassion. They are the definition of angels! In so many ways they represented the kindness shown by the many medical people who provided for my care. I will forever be indebted to all of them for their gifts of service provided me.

Miracle 6:

Transport Costs Covered

Fixed Wing
Learjet 45

Range: 2300 statute miles
Cruise Speed: 520 mph
Runway requirement: 4500 feet
Number of Patients: 2
Base of Operation: Anchorage, Fairbanks

Life Flight Lear 45 Jet: Flew Bruce from Fairbanks to Anchorage

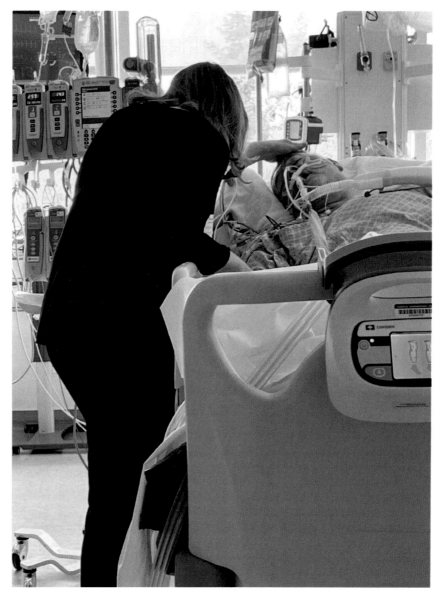

Bruce's wife, Roberta, giving comfort upon arrival in Anchorage with Bruce in a coma.

While I was unconscious at Fairbanks Hospital, they performed an emergency surgery because all my organs were failing. It was determined my colon had burst and sepsis, or septic shock, had set in to take me down. They realized they could not fully address the severity of my case and needed to get me to Anchorage ASAP.

The next day, they arranged a medivac airplane transport service to get me to Providence Hospital in Anchorage. A Lear 45 jet was used for the transport. Through modern flight-following services, called Flight Aware, my family was able to track the progress of the flight from departure to arrival. I am so grateful for the many prayers of family, friends, and acquaintances who were praying fervently for me.

A short time prior to the flight, a case manager at the hospital in Fairbanks called my family. She explained what was happening and that I was being air-lifted to Anchorage. The case worker also informed my family about a $50.00 insurance policy which could be bought to "help" defray some of the costs of the flight. The policy was wisely bought.

An exact cost was never presented to us, and to the best of our knowledge the cost of the flight was fully paid by the $50.00 insurance policy purchased.

Thank you Lord for the miracle of protection provided! I am so grateful that God used this wonderful caseworker, who had knowledge of this benefit and was willing to share it with my family.

Yes, this was an unbelievable miracle God used to bless me and my family.

Miracle 7:

Ostomy Bag

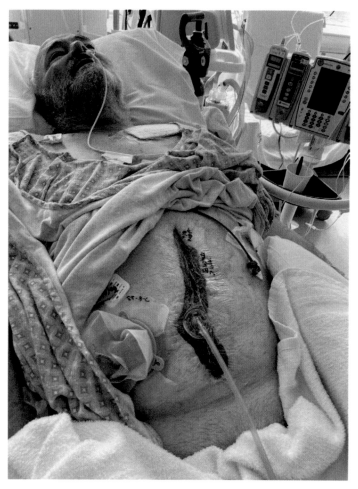

Ostomy Bag and Incision for multiple surgeries due to sepsis

My arrival at Providence Hospital in Anchorage resulted in three more abdominal surgeries in an attempt to stop the effects of sepsis. At one point, the doctors told my family they had done everything possible to clean out the infection and only time would tell about the results.

Would my damaged organs begin to work again?

During this critical seven to ten-day period, I was in a drug-induced coma. Once they quit giving me the drugs to keep me sedated, it took a while for me to awake. The delay in my coming out of the coma caused some real concern for my family.

Would I wake up? What would life look like even if I did wake up?

The truth was that my life was hanging in the balance, and there was no assurance of the outcome. Fortunately, I eventually woke up and started a two and a half-month hospital stay for recovery.

Those early days were difficult. With tubes and wires connected at every orifice of my body, it was difficult to speak more than a whisper. I could recognize family members, but then I would drift off into Lala-Land.

One of the actions taken by the doctors to preserve my life was to install an ostomy bag to address waste issues and keep it from further impacting my recovery. The installation of an ostomy bag changed the internal plumbing process of my digestive system, and it became a new way of dealing with life post-surgery. This process also resulted in a weight loss of fifty pounds.

I am grateful to the doctors for all the efforts they made on my behalf to save my life. The good news was that the ostomy allowed the doctors to save my life. The downside was that I had to learn how to navigate life with a bag to deal with waste matters.

During the two and a half-month hospital stay in Anchorage, getting the bag to stay attached to me was a major challenge. Because of several surgeries in the immediate area where the bag attaches to the skin, it was difficult to get a good seal. Consequently, there were days where specialty wound nurses would work diligently to reconnect it three to four times. It was a struggle, which was part of the whole recovery process.

It is hard to describe the helplessness and anxiety that went with living with an ostomy bag that was difficult to keep on. The bag was attached with adhesive flanges that would adhere to the skin. Occasionally, a paste-like material, much like plumber's putty, was used to additionally secure it. Sometimes, I would get lucky, and it would stay on for two, maybe three, days. Then, there would be days when it would need to be replaced three to four times during the day.

After two and a half months in the hospital, it was time to make the long flight from Anchorage to Dallas, TX, where I would begin further rehab. I was scheduled to be picked up by the cab in front of the hospital at 4:00 a.m. to get to the airport for a direct flight. At around 3:15-3:30 a.m., nurses and specialists were again struggling to get the bag secured. How was I going to survive an eight-hour direct flight ordeal without struggling to replace the bag myself!? To control the outflow, I had actually quit eating the night before and during the trip. Fortunately, my brother-in-law, Gerald Oliver, was traveling with me and was invaluable in helping me navigate the airports and the long flight. I made the trip uneventfully and was lucky to have had my bag stay on the whole time.

Upon my arrival at the rehab facility in Dallas, I was faced with finding adequate nursing care to help with the ostomy bag. Soon after arrival, a family member contacted a nurse, Kerri, who specialized in helping people with an ostomy. She became a special angel who helped me figure out how to keep the ostomy bag on. As simple as this sounds, she gave me a belt that went around me and was attached to each side of the bag. This added pressure was just the right amount to keep the bag on for a week at a time. I would proceed to see her weekly to have it changed, but what a mental and emotional relief it became to not worry as much as I had previously.

While in Alaska, I was told by the doctors that the ostomy could be reversed after six months. I was definitely relieved to know this fact and was already counting down the days that the procedure could happen.

As fate would have it or as part of God's plan, on December 12, 2023, almost six months to the day in Midlothian, Texas, I had Dr. Kandel operate and reverse the ostomy. I knew of the skills of Dr. Kandel because two years earlier, he had operated on my colon. To put me back together, he reopened the eleven-inch incision in my abdomen, hooked the plumbing back up, cleaned up scar tissue, and closed his work with twenty-seven staples!

When I reflect on the six-month journey of healing, I continue to have praise and thankfulness to God for his mercies of healing. I'm grateful that the reversal of the ostomy bag was an option. Life would have been very different if reversal was not an option. I continue to be amazed at how God has used all the angels of doctors and nurses, from Alaska to Texas, to minister to me physically. There have been so many miracles along this health journey that I can only say, "Thank you, God!"

Miracle 8:

Faith and Telling His Story

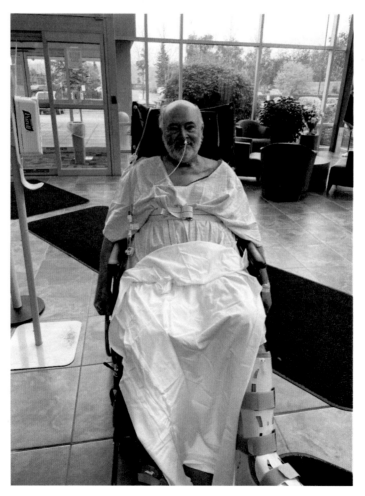

Bruce in a wheelchair at the lobby of St. Elias Specialty Hospital.

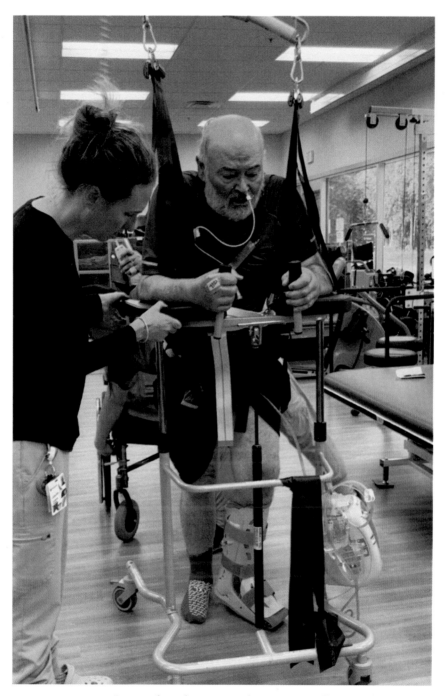

Bruce in sling relearning muscle memory to walk.

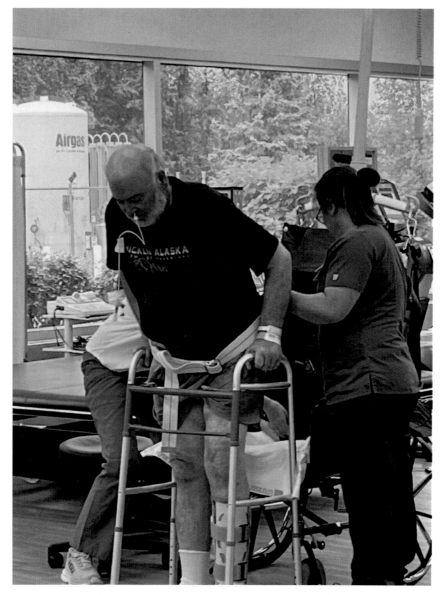

Bruce learning how to stand getting out of a wheelchair.

My Christian faith has been the bedrock of my being. My belief in the power of Jesus to forgive and give new life to anyone who believes in Him has been central to who I am.

Coming out of the coma from the accident brought lots of confusion as to where I was, why was I in such pain, and why couldn't I move or talk? The heavy sedation from the drug-induced coma eventually began to wear off. My mind became active, and I was able to start piecing things together as to what had happened.

Initially, there were feelings of regret at having been involved in such a senseless accident. There were questions like, would I ever get past all the physical pain I was dealing with!? Would I ever be able to walk, let alone ride a motorcycle?

At the center of all these questions was my faith in God. There were many nights when I was lying in bed, completely unable to move because of all the wires and tubes connected to me. It was during the quietness of the night that I would start praying to God.

Initially, there would be questions of God as to why this accident had happened. But eventually, I would get to my relationship with Jesus and start to feel a sense of peace.

At the core of my relationship with Jesus was the truth that He could be trusted, no matter the outcome of my accident. I could trust that my spiritual walk with Him was secured by the blood He shed on the cross for me.

At some point, in the midst of the prayers, I began to realize how blessed I was to be alive. There were so many things that could have ended my life or maimed me for life. Instead, I was alive, and, for the most part, it appeared I would have a chance at a full recovery. After much prayer, there came a peace that only God can give. In that peace, I was able to say that whatever the outcome, I was willing to praise Him. It was a surrender of my will to Him. I said, "God, I am willing to share this experience with whoever you want me to because it is really Your story."

The realization that God had spared my life caused a level of gratitude to God that I wanted to share with everyone. It was a newfound inspiration that I realized was part of His plan. In sparing my life, I could, in turn, share the many miracles that God performed as part of my Alaska journey. My life had changed, not just physically but also spiritually. The presence of God's Holy Spirit invaded my heart, and I had nothing but gratitude for Him. I wanted to share with others the blessings I had been given by God for physically saving my life.

The miracle of being given another chance at life has deepened my faith in God. It has given me a new purpose: to share God's miraculous power to perform miracles and be there in the face of life's tragedies. Without question, my experience is really His story of grace and mercy. I am just the actor who gets to tell the story.

Miracle 9:

Survival without Permanent Damage

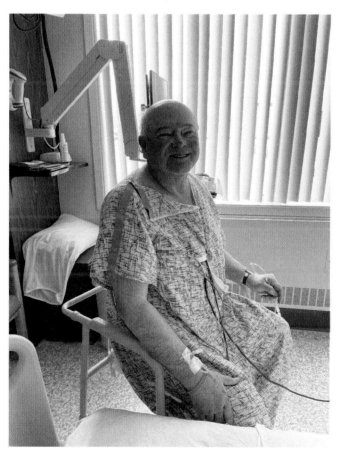

Bruce in Fairbanks Hospital the day after the accident and the day before sepsis set in from ruptured colon.

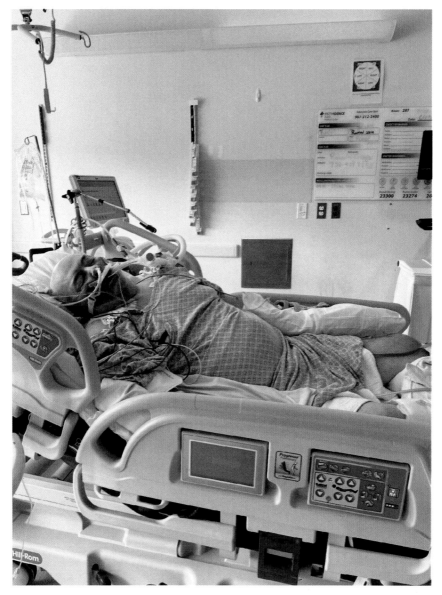

Bruce in coma in Anchorage with tubes and wires everywhere

Flying over the handlebars of a motorcycle at 65 mph is a recipe for disaster on a number of fronts. The biggest concern is just surviving and living to tell about it. The second concern is the ramifications of the accident. Is one going to have serious health issues like paralysis, a broken neck, a brain injury, or become permanently bedridden from the accident? These are inherent risks when choosing to ride a motorcycle, especially when experiencing a violent crash.

I recognize that not everyone who experiences the kind of violent motorcycle accident like I encountered has survived unscathed. Chances are that most have some kind of injury that has long-term effects.

I am fortunate that the injuries I sustained did not have a permanent effect on my ability to function. In addition to broken bones (i.e., clavicle, scapula, punctured lung, and ankle), the most serious impact for me was the sepsis I sustained from a ruptured colon.

One may ask, where is the miracle in all of this? As much as my injuries were able to be addressed and eventually brought under control, there were no long-term, life-altering effects that would change my ability in the future to resume a normal life.

While I do not know the statistics on the survival rates of an accident of this type, I am guessing there is a fair share of survivors who have been permanently maimed, if not deceased, as a result of a similar accident.

I am beyond grateful to God for His hand of protection over my life. While there has been a recovery and rehabilitation process, it is expected that I will be able to resume normal daily activities. As my father has said to me multiple times since the accident, "You are a walking miracle!" I give credit to God for all of His healing graces.

Miracle 10:

Hickel House

Hickel House of Providence Hospital in Anchorage

Immediately upon hearing of my accident, my immediate family began planning to come to Alaska. My wife and sister-in-law left as soon as possible to be with me. The first ten days, I was mostly in a coma. There was concern about whether I was going to survive the sepsis infection.

Alaska is a very expensive place to visit and stay. When my wife had to immediately rush to my side, she had to do the normal things like rent a car and book a hotel. Those costs in the first few days were merely insane.

In the few ensuing days, God opened up a room at the Hickel House, a motel owned and attached to Providence Hospital. It was very much like a Ronald McDonald house. Its purpose is to provide reasonable housing costs for family members visiting loved ones in the hospital. The cost of the room was comparable to a mid-market hotel.

Because of its proximity to the hospital and its reasonable pricing, the hotel is in strong demand. In the scramble to find a place to stay, miraculously, within twenty-four hours of my being at the Providence Hospital, a room opened, and my family was able to secure it. Between my family members and the friends who came to be with me, someone was at the Hickel House every night for seventy-two days. What a miraculous opportunity the housing was for all the people who came to be with me.

I work for a real estate company in Chicago, NAI Hiffman. I am privileged to work with great people. During my entire accident ordeal, my company stepped up big-time to assist my family. They provided funds for some airline tickets, as well as picking up the cost of the Hickel house for the full seventy-two days! This is a huge financial commitment that they graciously covered. I can't begin to say how much I appreciated their generosity, but more importantly, the meaning of saying they cared.

Does God not watch out for His loved ones? Yes, he does! Having the convenience of the Hickel house and NAI Hiffman covering the cost is amazing and miraculous. I do remember when I was told by my family that their housing was being paid for by my company. I cried tears of unbelief at the provisions God provided!

Miracle 11:

Family and Friends

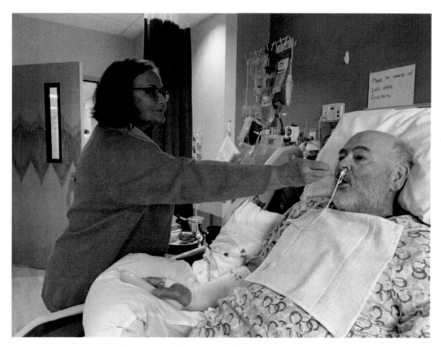

Bruce being fed by sister Carolyn Fitzsimons

During the entire time I was in the hospital in Alaska, which was seventy-two days, a family member and three special friends came, and someone was with me every day. During this period, a plan was put in place for a family member and these special friends to rotate into Alaska to be with me, usually each spending about a week's time. My three sisters are Kathy Oliver, Connie McRill, and Carolyn Fitzimmons. My sister-in-law, Sheree McCullough, came the first week I was in a coma. As I neared the end of the hospital stay, my brother-in-law, Gerald Oliver, came, spent time with me, and eventually assisted me in traveling back to the "lower 48," as was the popular expression.

In addition to my family coming to Alaska, three of my friends came as well. Randall Davey, Floyd Hoffman, and Mike Bear. One weekend, Randall walked into my room, having flown in from Phoenix just to be with me. What a morale booster it was to see him early in the recovery process. Our friendship goes back to college days and many adventures since then.

Floyd Hoffman was a college friend that I shared a love of motorcycles with even back in college. At Mount Vernon Nazarene University, we were the only two with motorcycles. Several years ago, we shared a ride in Colorado together. Our friendship has spanned more than fifty years. Floyd wanted to come and be with me. I marveled at how he would ride the local bus to and from the hospital and Hickel House with some of the unsavory characters from the town.

The other friend that came and spent time with me was Mike Bear. Mike and his family grew up in the same church as my wife in Bucyrus, Ohio. It wasn't until Mike came to Olivet Nazarene University as a student that I got to know him, since I was teaching there at the time. Over the years, we have maintained our friendship and stayed in touch. Mike also raised his hand and said he wanted to come.

I remember one particular time when Mike took Dr. MacNeal aside and advocated for my needs. I was so grateful for his presence. I enjoyed the conversations and relished the time we spent together. Both Mike and Floyd were always willing to go with me to the physical therapy room and watch the therapist put me through the paces. They both were encouraging as I struggled to regain some of my life skills, like walking, climbing stairs, and riding a bike.

I was blessed by the care provided by my family and friends. Each one of these people provided unbelievable support, not just being there for me but talking to doctors and nurses to make sure I got the necessary resources. Each one provided the miraculous support I needed at just the right time. Each one advocated on my behalf when I was not capable.

Early on, and shortly after coming out of the coma, my sister, Kathy Oliver, was there to spend a couple weeks with me. During this time, I was in an extreme amount of pain and was still phasing in and out of the coma. During those times, I felt a lot of darkness and confusion and was still trying to figure out what was going on. However, there were numerous times when I would wake up, and I would see my sister's face at the foot of the bed and feel a sense of calm because of her presence. How miraculous that God could use family and friends to give me hope.

Following the coma, I was in the hospital for approximately ten weeks. During this time, I continued to become more aware and cognizant of what was going on. Because I had a family member or friend(s) with me each week, it was miraculous to see how each of them helped me in dealing with my medical issues and talking with doctors and nurses.

What was more miraculous was that each of the family members and friends were able to travel to Alaska. Getting to Alaska takes a lot of effort, with flights usually stopping in Seattle before continuing northwest to Anchorage. The efforts each person made to be with me often left me in tears as I realized their efforts were in love and support of me.

Several of my sisters used social media to keep many friends and family informed of my changing status. The result was the prayers of many people for me. A go-fund-me page was set up to help defray the many costs of the accident. I cried when I saw the volume of people who cared enough to donate.

Thank you to each person who contributed.

My family and friends that were with me in the hospital got to see the pain, struggles, agony, and challenges I faced in the recovery process. Since they each had a "rink-side" seat to observe the process, I have asked those who felt inclined to share their experiences. Below are a few of their varied reactions.

Comments from Family and Friends:
Bryan Barus: (Riding partner)

Bruce, when you told me you were thinking of riding a motorcycle back to Alaska, I was honored that you even thought of including me on your journey. I was excited to be a part of it.

Since I didn't have the time to ride to and from Alaska, we decided to have you drive and trailer the bikes while I flew into Fairbanks. It was easy to travel to Fairbanks. I had a good night's sleep, and I was very excited for the next day.

The morning of our departure, June 17, 2023, was a crisp, beautiful morning around 50°, a perfect day for riding. After getting out of Fairbanks you graciously waived me into the lead. It was awesome, as I was experiencing Alaska for the first time.

About an hour into the journey, I was leading, and you were approximately half a mile in trail. I saw signs for a scenic turnout and decided that it was a great place to take our first stop, check our gear, and take in God's beauty.

The scenic turnout had two entrances, the first obscured by a tall stand of trees and the second on a straightaway. Not wanting to take the first one, as I'm always fearful of trucks pulling trailers, I decided to take the second one. As I decelerated, I turned left into the parking lot, and I looked up and noticed you were entering the turn. I started to put my kickstand down, and I was fumbling as I looked down to see what was going on. I lost sight of you, but then looked back up after I heard the beginning of your crash. I did not see it start, but I saw the middle and the end. The end was a little surreal. After you separated from your motorcycle, you actually got up, took a few steps, and then collapsed. Realizing what happened, I started to make my way toward you.

There was another couple at the scenic turnout. I asked the wife to go flag traffic at the curve while the husband was racing toward you as well. I was nervous that someone would come around the corner, not see you, and run you over. It turns out that the location of the accident was actually a good thing. We were able to re-route traffic around the accident by using the two entrances of the scenic overview.

Shortly after I got to you, along with a fellow bystander, the first car to arrive was driven by a recent off-duty EMT. His name was Ryan. He was on his way home from work. He parked his car in a defensive position, grabbed his trauma bag, and immediately went to work taking care of you.

We did not have cell phone service. Ryan had a special first responder's phone and was able to call for EMS support (Emergency Medical Support). While he was doing that, I was looking for your Garmin Inreach GPS unit to possibly use that to call for help. EMS was only twenty-five minutes away, and the ambulance crew was just coming on duty. The crew was staffed with a medic.

In a very short time, after the first paramedic arrived, there were two Air Force paramedic troupers who also showed up. I did not catch their names. They were outstanding at what they did. I think they honestly made a difference beyond basic understanding. They were very methodical, comforting, and exhibited a lot of forethought in how to treat you. They were fantastic and consummate professionals. I'm glad we have young men like this protecting our country.

I was incredibly impressed with your presence of mind. Even though you went through some traumatic times and were arguably in shock at some level, you kept your wits about you. You engaged in conversation with us. When we asked you questions, you answered, and you kept your composure.

Sorry, I had to cut your riding gear and base layers off of you. I know those were important pieces of equipment to you. But at least I got to use my scissors :-)

Eventually, the EMS people arrived, and the volunteers did a successful handoff of you, putting you on a board and loading you into the ambulance. After loading you in the ambulance, they had some difficulty locating a vein to administer pain medication. That took an extra ten-plus minutes to get you situated before the ambulance started moving.

The ER team, the trauma surgeon, and the entire nursing team were fantastic. They did the best they could with the resources they had, and their skills made you comfortable and kept you alive.

Meanwhile, I was engaged with the Alaskan State trooper, working out the details for his report. It was at this time that I met Michael and Tanya, a phenomenal young couple with two young children. They introduced themselves, explained their motorcycle travel history, and offered their help.

Michael and Tanya are from Australia. They had been riding their motorcycles in Tanzania when Tanya experienced a crash. They knew exactly what you and I were going through. She shared the story of how others helped her in her time of need, and she and Michael were here to help you and me in our time of need. Michael was the manager of the local goldmine. They were on their way to the city of TOK, Alaska to buy a motorcycle. They offered to pick up your motorcycle and take it to their home in Fairbanks. I accepted their offer.

As the ambulance made its way to Fairbanks, I unloaded your most valuable personal items off your bike and loaded them onto mine (i.e., computer, GPS, wallet, phone, watch, passport, etc.). It was about an hour's ride back to Fairbanks.

I was able to take your truck and trailer to Michael's house the following day, on Father's Day, interrupting his time with his family, to retrieve your bike. Again, their intervention was much needed and much appreciated.

Here are some observations from the crash and the crash location. You were riding on brand new tires with less than a couple hundred miles. They were fifty-fifty tires, and we were on asphalt. It was early morning, and there may have been some moisture on the pavement. It was a curve, and the road was banked. The view into the curve was obstructed by the trees. There was brand new asphalt that had just been recently placed, and the asphalt had an oily residue.

When discussing the accident with you in the hospital the following day, you thought maybe you were carrying a little extra speed into the curve. You may have been distracted while sightseeing and looking at all of the beauty. But most importantly, your cruise control did not disengage. I don't think you can point at one thing that caused the crash, but it was rather a confluence of many variables.

At the hospital, in spite of the trauma, you appeared in really good shape. You were remarkably well, given the circumstances, and in good spirits. The nursing team and the doctors were all talking about the next phase, which was simply watching your recovery for a few days to make sure you were stable enough to travel by airplane. I believe they were worried about embolisms.

On Sunday, you had multiple phone calls with your wife and sisters. We worked hard to figure out the details and all of the next steps. It was awesome to witness the love that your family has for each other. You are important to many people and loved by all.

Given all that we knew, we decided that the next course of action was for me to drive the truck and trailer with the bikes back to Chicago. I started my journey Monday morning. On my way home on Monday, I took some time to stop in Tok and ride to Chicken, Alaska, and back. I'm glad I did. On Monday, multiple texting phone calls to you went unanswered.

Tuesday morning, when I woke, I called the ICU looking for an update, and that's when they informed me that things had taken a turn for the worse. An emergency surgery was required, and the situation was touch and go.

When I heard the news, I immediately wanted to turn around and drive to Anchorage. Robbi adjusted her travel plans, and instead of flying to Fairbanks, she flew to Anchorage. Your sister, Kathy, convinced me there was nothing I could do and I should continue my trip home.

Candidly, I had a feeling that I had abandoned you. I knew you were in excellent hands with the medical team, the flight team, and everyone else around you, but I couldn't help but feel I should have been there by your side in your greatest time of need. I'm sorry, I wasn't.

I made the return trip to Chicago in almost complete silence, except for the occasional phone call. I left early Monday morning and returned late Friday night. It was a lot of driving. While I can remember some of it, most of it was just a blur. I enjoyed the solitude and the opportunity to be disconnected from civilization. I was anxious to know how you were doing. The occasional text from Kathy was my only source of news. While I was hoping and praying for the best, I couldn't help but occasionally think of the worst.

I'm convinced your faith, family, and friends made all the difference in the world.

I'm glad you're still with us!!

Kathy Oliver (sister)

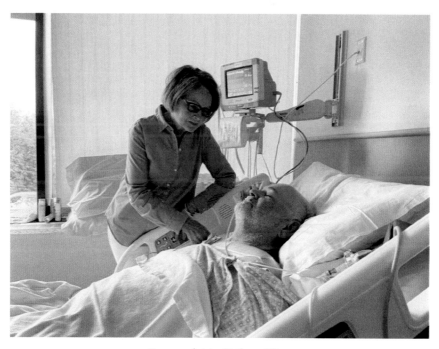

Bruce and sister Kathryn Oliver

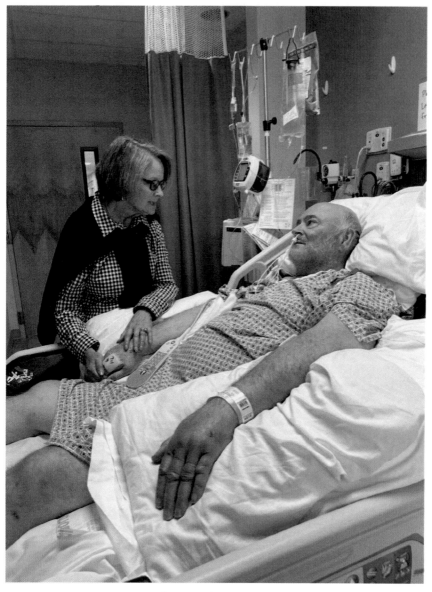

Bruce in coma and sister Kathryn Oliver watching over him.

"Faith does not operate in the realm of the possible. There is no glory for God in that which men can do. Faith begins where man's power ends."

—George Mueller

"On June 17, 2023, we started a faith journey on behalf of Bruce's life! A healthy body was out of the realm of possibility, and our 'power' ended. There was nothing left to do but PRAY . . . and trust God . . . with the outcome.

In all my faith journeys in life, I have to say that it has never felt good! But God . . . the sovereign Lord God, does some of His best work when I am the most powerless, the most bewildered, helpless, and scared. This 'faith journey' with Bruce was no exception. It was hard with difficult and discouraging days . . . often times not knowing if he would live or die. But God . . . had a plan! 'A plan for good and not for evil, to give Bruce a future and a hope.'

"What is impossible with man is possible with God!"

Bruce's story is all about God . . . and bringing glory to God for working in his life in so many ways that were impossible with man. God has grown my faith and allowed me the privilege of sitting in a front row seat in awe of His divine hand working in Bruce's life.

My faith has grown! I can say with confidence that God is good. And it is okay when life falls apart, as long as I am walking with Him! I don't like to think about how I would have responded if Bruce had gone to heaven (he was ready), but I hope and pray that I would let God be God!!

I would keep on walking the 'journey of faith' one day at a time . . . until six months, a year, or two years later, I fall on my knees and marvel at the power and glory of God! Bruce's life and his story are not about him. It is all about God!

Whoever is reading this and going through a hard time, I encourage you to keep on . . . keeping on . . . traveling your 'faith journey' knowing that God is God. He will do what is best to bring glory to God out of your situation, just as he has done for Bruce."

Connie McRill (sister)

Bruce in St. Elias Specialty Hospital with sister Connie McRill. Notice scar on left shoulder to put in plates, pins, and screws to repair the shoulder.

"I'll never forget the day…Saturday, June 17, 2023! It held for me one of those dreaded phone calls, when you never forget where you were and what you were doing. My dad and siblings were on edge, knowing Bruce was on his third motorcycle trip on the Alaskan Highway. I anxiously answered the call from my sister, Kathy. Her first words were, "Bruce has been in a bad accident, but he's alive!" I took a deep breath, as I realized one of my greatest fears was unfolding. We, his family, were acutely aware of Bruce's absolute oneness between he and his massive machine, Crazy. Without hesitation, he never got on her without suiting up with the best gear in the industry. He was always alert and focused upon all that was going on in the immediate vicinity, as well as ahead.

However, on this fateful day, the unexpected happened! Over the next several months in Fairbanks Memorial Hospital, Providence Alaskan Medical Center, and St. Elias Specialty Hospital, in Anchorage, Bruce fought for his life. Sepsis, broken bones, and severe pain wracked his entire body. Immediately, his family and friends rallied to his side.

As I processed the life- threatening reality that my brother's life was hanging in the balance and he was so very far away from his family. I couldn't imagine not being there for him. I am lucky to be part of a very close-knit family with sibling bonds far more connected than most. I booked a ticket to make my way out of the lower 48 to be with him. I always dreamed of seeing Alaska, just not under these circumstances.

Upon arriving in Anchorage that summer day, I went directly to St. Elias Specialty Hospital. This facility for acute care was the next step on his journey. The realization set in for all of us, just how grueling and unbelievably difficult the recovery days ahead would be! Kathy and I overlapped for several days with Bruce, as our days were consumed with care and advocacy for him. I became acutely aware of the weighty load I felt in standing vigil beside his bed.

Over the course of the next ten days, I fell into the daily routine of Ubering from Providence Hickel House at 8:00 AM to St. Elias across town. As I walked into Bruce's room, I'll never forget the sweet smile on his face each morning.

Here are some random memories that stick with me:

- The heartbreaking reality of seeing my brother in such a helpless condition. After all, he was the strong one who was always there first to help and support others.

- I would stand by his bed much of the day, gently gripping his hands, massaging his fingers, and helping his attempt to raise his arm off the bed.

- I would bring him a soft, warm washcloth to wash his face in the morning (thinking that must feel so good). After three or four days, he looked at me and said, "Could you bring me a COLD washcloth?" You just never know!

- As PT came for the first time to get him up out of bed, with tears in my eyes, I painstakingly watched the brutal struggle of rehabilitation process begin. I remember thinking, "This is going to be a long journey back! What does the journey look like, being so very far away from home and family?"

- As Bruce couldn't raise his arms to feed himself, I would feed him. He had no appetite, and each bite was a struggle to get down. Sometimes it was only two or three bites at a meal. We tried to bribe him with high protein milkshakes and ice cream, but even those often went untouched. And we ALL know how much he loves ice cream!

- Oh, how I remember his first wheelchair ride outside to get a breath of fresh air! That was a big moment, but with the broken ribs, he certainly winced at each bump in the sidewalk.

- I struggled leaving Bruce's side each evening around 6:00-7:00 pm. I just didn't want him to feel alone. As I'd stroke his right hand, I would pray over him, asking our Mighty Jehovah-Rapha to bring healing to his "broken body" and give him good rest for the night. Often, the only words were, "Oh God, we need YOU!"

- With Bruce, sick and tortured with pain, barely able to whisper, I observed something so special. Without fail, Bruce would kindly thank each doctor, nurse, technician or therapist for such good care. A forced, but genuine smile would cross his face and he whispered. "Thank you so much for your help!" He would often turn the focus to them, asking about their day, their families, or hobbies. Always thinking of others and spreading the love of Jesus!

- I remember holding the phone for him to say a few words to a friend or family member, only to hear him say, "You talk." Spurts of energy were scarce.

As the day approached for my return home, I was dreading telling him goodbye, knowing it would be one of the most difficult things I'd ever done. When Carolyn came, we had a couple days there together with Bruce in the "changing of the guards". I walked briskly out of that facility to catch my Uber to the airport. Tears were streaming down my face as I was praying, "Lord, he is yours, please take care of him!"

A week later, at home in my living room having my devotions, I knelt at the couch crying desperately for God to intervene on Bruce's behalf. It was that guttural, wordless cry…surrendering MY BROTHER to Him. Pleading for what I humanly wanted, yet surrendering Bruce to whatever would bring the most glory to God and His Kingdom! That was a turning point for me in this whole journey with Bruce and his accident. Nothing happens in our lives without passing through the Father's hands. I knew I could trust Him to "write this story…for His glory".

Now, nine months later, I continue to marvel at God's plan! His miraculous touch has been on Bruce's body, mind, and spirit! I am praising God for His faithfulness and provision. It is HIS STORY, for sure!

Bruce, I love you and am so grateful I can still pick up my phone and call you! Thanks for sharing your journey with everyone you meet, pointing us all to Jesus! To God Be the Glory!!!!

This is the verse God gave in the midst of the crisis: "Because he loves me, says the Lord, I will rescue him, for he acknowledges My Name." Psalm 91:14"

Randall Davey: (friend)

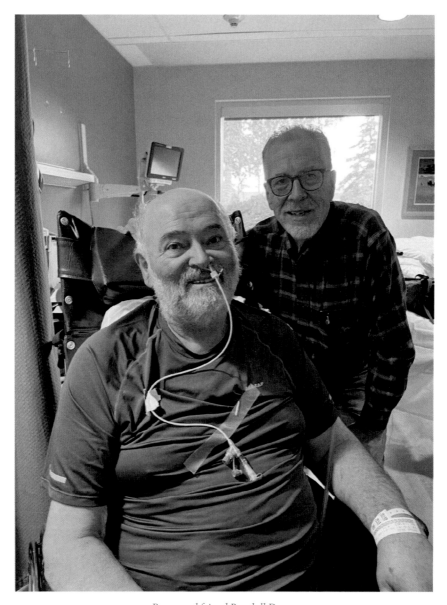

Bruce and friend Randall Davey

"On our first call after the accident, you said, "Randy, just a few weeks ago, I was pitching forty-pound bales of hay. Today, I cannot hold my phone or feed myself." I got off that call and started searching for flights. It was not a question as to whether I would go. It was only a question of when. When I walked into your room at St. Elias Specialty Hospital, I realized your voice betrayed your condition. I have always known you to be a mountain of a man, strong as an ox, able to leap tall buildings. To see you broken beyond imagination defied comprehension. To watch you grimace in pain when the nurses hoisted you from the bed to your wheelchair was difficult to watch.

Fortunately, for both of us, your sister Carolyn was there. I found great solace in talking to her, and we both agreed that the one thing you had going for you—the thing that has been your strong suit through the ages—is what I call 'Granger Grit.' I returned home believing that you would be in Alaska for months. I listened as the nurses talked about the stages of progress you would have to realize to get back on your feet, a goal I knew you would reach but not in the record time you did.

Thanks be to God for your commitment to recovery and devotion to the Lord, who was and is present in every dimension of your life. Alaska 2023—I will never forget. Randall"

Floyd Hoffman: (friend)

Bruce and friend Floyd Hoffman

"I always enjoy your adventures, especially the ones I have ridden with you. When you decided to make another trip to Alaska, I decided to go along with you remotely. You gave me the URL to go online and follow your GPS tracks as you made your way to Fairbanks, Alaska, pulling your trailer with your bike and Bryan Barus's bike. You left around June 10th, 2023, planning on taking five days to get to Fairbanks, where you were to pick Bryan up at the airport. It was enjoyable checking your progress every day as you headed west and then north to Alaska. However, on Saturday, June 17th, the day you were to leave for the Arctic Ocean, I was not able to see any new tracks. I was hoping everything was okay and that you were on the road, and I would eventually be able to pick up the GPS tracks again.

On Sunday afternoon, June 18, I was at home, watching TV when my phone rang. I saw on the screen that the call was from you, or at least your phone. I remember answering in some lighthearted way, thinking I was talking to you. Then Bryan's voice came through, telling me it was not you. Right away, my stomach jumped to my throat, knowing that you were supposed to be on the road on the motorcycle, and why was Bryan calling me on your phone?! I got up from my seat and started to head for the bedroom, not wanting Arlene to hear what I feared was very bad news.

Well, it was bad news, but not as bad as I initially feared. Bryan told me about the accident but said that you had remained conscious the whole time. He stated you were in the Fairbanks hospital, in stable condition, and would probably be released within a week or less. Of course, the motorcycle part of the trip was over, and Bryan was planning on driving your car and trailer with the bikes back to Illinois. I think Bryan headed for Illinois on Monday, and all seemed to be as good as could be expected under the circumstances.

Then Tuesday, June 19th came. Your doctors discovered that you had a ruptured colon and it had been poisoning your body since the accident the previous Saturday. Later, I would learn you were fighting sepsis big time. Bryan kept me informed as best he could while on the road back to Illinois. One of your sisters kept friends and family informed through Facebook. For a few days, things were kind of a blur from my perspective due to a lack of information and misinformation that began to circle on the grapevine.

I knew things were very serious, and I feared for your life, as many other friends and family did also.

You were air-evacuated to a bigger hospital in Anchorage. You got to ride in a beautiful jet aircraft that I'm sure your aviator's background would have loved, but you were aware of none of it at the time. Many prayers were going out for you, and I feared that I may lose one of my best friends ever.

By the next week, things were looking much better for you, but still very serious. We all knew by then that your stay in Alaska was going to be a little longer than the week we were first told. With that in mind, your family put a plan together to make sure you were never left without some family support during your stay there. Your wife, Robbi, and her sister were the first family to arrive in Anchorage to be with you. Your amazing sisters then set up a schedule so that one of them, or Robbi, would be with you at all times.

By mid-July, we knew that your stay was going to be kind of indefinite. One night, Arlene and I were talking about your situation, and she said that maybe I should just go out to Anchorage and spend some time with you and help out in any way I could. Following Arlene's always wise thoughts and suggestions, I called your sister Kathy and offered to help relieve the family for a week or two if that would help. They graciously accepted my offer, and I made arrangements to arrive on August 4th and stay through August 12th.

I was excited to see Anchorage, but not under those circumstances. I was even more excited to see you and to be able to help my friend in any way. That first day I walked into your room at the St. Elias Specialty Hospital was a real awakening for me. It was so good to see you and to know that you were alive and expecting a full, but slow, recovery.

As I greeted you by your bedside, we both shed some happy and grateful tears. I'm not sure if I had seen you in some other situation that I would have known it was you. You had lost so much weight, you had a full beard, and the stress of what you had gone through physically and mentally was showing on your weary face. You certainly did not look like the young seventy-two-year-old man that I had last seen in Illinois.

Robbi was still there and helped me get oriented and settled into my room at the hospital guest house called Hickel House. I could tell from Robbi's countenance that she was very concerned about you and your future recovery and wanted to do all that she could to help you.

My first full day with you brought more unexpected revelations. I was amazed at how weak you were. It was a struggle for you to even turn on your side in bed. Getting out of bed to eat or go to the bathroom was even more of a struggle. I had to help you swing your legs over the edge of the bed and almost pick you up to get you into a wheelchair. It made me very aware of how fragile our bodies can be and how quickly we can lose our strength and stamina when subjected to stress like you went through.

What was amazing was how much progress you made in the eight days I was with you. By the time your friend, Mike Bear, arrived to replace me, you were pretty much able to get out of bed on your own. You were walking around the hall for two to three laps at a time. You were climbing the stairs in the physical therapy room. And your appearance changed too, thanks to the barber that I was able to get to come into your room for a haircut and beard trim. By the time Mike showed up, I felt that it may be only a matter of time before you would be able to make it back to the lower forty-eight states.

I know all of this has undoubtedly been the most traumatic experience that you have ever been through. But I know and have seen how it has drawn you closer to our Lord and how it has been a blessing and inspiration to friends and many people that you have never met and don't even know. You have been a blessing to me. I consider those days I spent with you in Anchorage to be some of the most precious and rewarding days of my life. God's plans are always perfect. Isn't it amazing how He takes some of the worst things that we go through and makes them a blessing for us and many others?

One final thought. I know that you have talked about hanging up the riding gear and not wanting to put your family and friends through anything like this again. I also know how much you have enjoyed riding in the past and how that was such a big part of your life. You have an adventurous spirit, and I don't think that ever goes away in a person like you or me. As we age and our priorities and abilities change, we adjust, but that spirit is always there. We just satisfy it in different and modified ways. With that in mind, let me leave you with two quotes that I recently heard and wrote down while watching the movie "Tuck Everlasting."

"Don't be afraid of death. Be afraid of the life unlived."
"You don't have to live forever. You just have to live."

"I love you, my brother!"

Mike Bear: (friend)

Bruce and friend Mike Bear

"I received a call from you telling me you were in a nasty bike wreck, but you were going to be okay. Little did I know things would change dramatically shortly after that call.

So many times, someone has a need, and we say, "Let me know if I can help," but realistically, either we never can or life doesn't allow. This time, I had the time and means to actually do something. Between your sisters and Roberta, a date range was established when I could help. Floyd went first, and I followed Floyd. I remember the conversation with Roberta about the differences between having family (wife and sisters) there and guys. Guys are not wired to be as nurturing as girls and when guys are cared for by guys, I think that dynamic is different too. There is some base male DNA-driven perspective and interaction that just sees and does things differently. We tend to push each other a little more just by being men.

A short time later, I found myself in Alaska. I have never stayed somewhere (hospital hotel facility) where the warning sign on the exit said, "Beware of Moose!" Floyd gave me the tour upon arrival and passed the 'watch torch' on to me.

Next morning was the beginning of my stay. I really didn't know what to expect. In some ways, you were in better shape than I expected, while in other ways, not as much. From a 10,000-foot perspective, I felt my 'presence' was more a commitment to making sure the hospital knew there was someone 'watching' what was going on. Certainly, my support of you and your needs was my function. But my purpose was to let the people taking care of you know that someone outside the 'circle' was paying attention. Although I believe the staff there was fantastic in function, professionalism, process, and personality, there is something to be said for the presence of an engaged person paying attention to what's happening.

I remember years ago when our daughter Emily was in the hospital. Marcia or I were there 24/7. There were other kids in the hospital at the same time. Emily received better care, more attention, and was treated better than the same-age kids without parents because we were there. We asked questions and were supportive and friendly to the staff. It was important to be respectful but to also hold them accountable. There were times we would make a stand and draw lines not to be crossed. Clearly, our presence makes all the difference. This experience helped prepare me to be present for you.

I helped you think through your next steps. Questions like where to go after the hospital? What needed to happen for you physically in order for you to have confidence mentally? What were the next steps? I mostly listened. I let you hear your own thoughts; maybe, applied a little logic and perspective in the process.

Bruce, if I did help, I think it was that I was able to better articulate your concerns and needs to the staff from a timeline standpoint. I'm not sure calling me an advocate would be correct, as I believe you had some wonderful staff members who wanted the best for you. I think after you are someone's patient for a period of time, perspectives can become jumbled. What I did was to help unjumble information for you and the staff. Hopefully, I helped with fears, needs, and realities for you and the staff to assist in coming up with a plan.

Memories? The PT (physical therapy) activities surrounding that place were amazing! Your progress as well as the people going through PT hardships were amazing. I thought the OT (occupational therapy) area in the kitchen was really cool! Asking you to make a grilled cheese sandwich. What a great real-life determination of skill level and a taste of difficulties to come, so you'd be mentally prepared. Your occupational therapist, Kathleen, was so special. After work, she volunteered to show me the city. She toured me around Anchorage, where I saw Baluga whales, the statue of Captain Cook, and had dinner with her.

I also remember feeling like I was getting the opportunity to be supportive of Roberta. Although we've had a great relationship over the years, I have a special connection to her. She was part of my early years in Bucyrus, Ohio. We grew up in the same town and at the same church. I think she actually was my babysitter once or twice when we lived on Walnut Street. Her family was part of my growing up, from her Aunt Miss Mable, to attending high school with her Sister Sheree.

While spending time with you in the hospital, I also remember a strong feeling that you needed to finish your Alaska trip. Maybe that's a projection on my part—who knows? It may not necessarily be on a bike, but I felt like there was an open chapter you needed to complete for closure. I'm sure a visit to St. Elias is in order to visit the Drs., Annie, Kathleen, and the PT/OT people.

In conclusion, I remember leaving feeling like I finally had the chance to help. Being served is a blessing. Being able to serve is a privilege. Thanks for that opportunity." Mike.

Bruce and Gerald Oliver, brother-in-law, enjoying a sandwich at Portillos in Dallas.

Miracle 12:

Travel Arrangements Gifted

Stephanie Nelson Warner, my cousin's daughter who works for Alaska Airlines

Getting to Alaska is a challenge, no matter what part of the country one is coming from. Airline tickets are expensive. Ironically, my cousin's daughter, Stephanie Nelson Warner, works for Alaska Airlines. With her access to discount tickets, she was able to assist various family members in getting to and from Alaska. Her kindness and generosity enabled my family to save lots of money on travel costs.

My company, NAI Hiffman, was also generous with airline tickets. The most critical contribution they made was providing two first-class tickets to me and a helper to make the trip from Alaska back to the states. My brother-in-law, Gerald Oliver, came and provided valuable travel support. Having his support was such a gift, as he helped provide the extra energy and strength needed to get me through the airport and onto the airplane. The first-class tickets were such a welcomed gift.

The first-class tickets also came as a much-needed luxury. While in the hospital in Alaska, there was a constant struggle to keep the ostomy bag on me. Sometimes, the bag would fail three to four times a day, with specially trained personnel working hard to keep it attached. Even in the early morning hours before the flight out of Alaska, nurses were struggling to keep the bag attached. How was I going to make it eight to ten hours on an airplane with the bag staying attached? To aid in this process, I had stopped eating and drinking any food or water twelve hours before the flight. I also prayed a lot that I would be able to make it through the long flight without any additional drama of the bag coming off. Fortunately, the comfort of the first-class ticket provided by my company helped make the trip much more manageable.

The day came when it was time to leave Providence Hospital for the airplane ride to Dallas, Texas. I left my hospital bed at 4:00 a.m. to uber to the airport in Anchorage, AK. The flight to Dallas, TX, was an eight-hour flight. I was to continue four more months of rehabilitation and further medical care in Dallas.

The flight was taxing on my energy level, as my endurance and strength were marginal.

Fortunately, having the first-class seat(s) enabled me to relax with the extra room for the long flight. I was able to make it through the entire flight without any incident. This was truly a miracle. I was so grateful to NAI Hiffman for providing this luxury upgrade.

How comforting and amazing it was to know of the help provided to my family. Without the support of Stephanie and NAI Hiffman, I know the logistics would have been much more difficult. What wonderful people stepped up and provided for me and my family! These angels of mercy provided such valuable gifts.

Miracle 13:

Hospital Staff and Workers

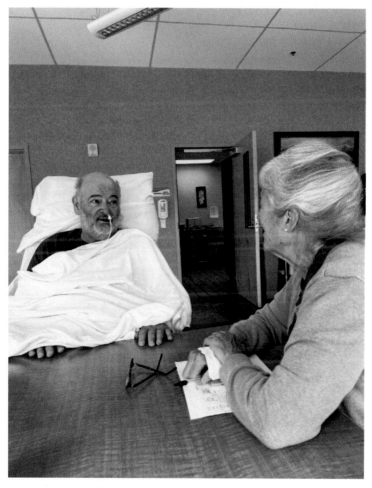

St. Elias Caseworker Annie stopping by to say Hi.

Bruce and Physical Therapist walking the halls of the hospital.

As the days and weeks of being in the hospital rolled on, I realized how blessed I was by the superb medical care I received. Many hospital workers come to Alaska to work for a set period of time, like six to twelve months as a contract worker. I realized these people were motivated to be there, and all of them were exceptionally talented and greatly aided in the speed of my recovery.

As I became more aware, I realized there were some special doctors and nurses that I wanted to gift one of my previous books. I had my assistant send me ten books, and I gave them away to those people God impressed me to give them to. One of the people was a young nurse who had just been baptized the Sunday before I met her. She was so excited about her faith, and it was fun to give her a copy of my book, which included stories of faith.

One of the people I gave a book to was Annie, the case worker at the St. Elias Specialty Hospital. Annie was reading the book, and every day she would come in smiling about one of the chapters she had just read. It was refreshing to me to know someone was reading my book and finding enjoyment in it. My prayer is that God will use those stories for His purpose.

One of the amazing miracles of this accident is how God used the various medical people to aid in my recovery. After coming out of the coma, I realized I couldn't move much in the bed because of all the tubes, wires, and apparatuses that were connected to me. I knew the recovery was going to be challenging and difficult. Every step along the way, it seemed God provided just the right paramedic, nurse, physical therapist, occupational therapist, and doctor to guide my recovery.

The medical team was clearly invested in helping me with the recovery. A staff person was always there to assist me, encourage me, and motivate me to keep pressing forward.

One of the physical therapists was a young lady, diminutive in size but with a huge attitude of "can-do." I did not have a choice about whether I was going to participate or not! If I were to have a forty-five-minute physical therapy session and there were five minutes left, you could count on her pushing me to do exercises for that time period. There were times after the workout sessions where I would fall back into bed, completely exhausted by the workout I had experienced. After the exhaustion would wear off, I would be so thankful for the physical progress I had made because this lady had pushed me to my limits.

The doctors who were responsible for my care were focused on providing me with the best care possible. They would take the time to discuss the pressing issues and the treatment options to be implemented. They were willing to give their time to explain things, and they showed genuine care. I often would pass them in the hall while doing physical therapy, like relearning the muscle memory of how to walk, and I would get encouraging comments from them.

Because many of the medical team members were contract workers, I felt like I had quality people providing me services because they were intentionally there to do their job. It takes a hearty soul to pull up stakes and go to Alaska to work. I was the gracious recipient of their generosity and encouragement. I know that without their help, I would not have made as speedy a recovery as I did. There were times they would be pulling the wound vac off of me, and they knew I was wincing from the pain. They would genuinely apologize for causing the pain and I would appreciate their sensitivity and awareness to respect my concerns. While this is not always a given in the medical field, I was blessed by many caregivers who did genuinely care. The level of medical care I received throughout the whole experience was miraculous.

A miracle on a much broader scale is the care I was provided at both Providence and St. Elias Specialty hospitals. Both of these are world-class hospitals, and I felt like I got nothing less than the best service while there. I later found out that I was admitted to the St. Elias rehab facility when there was a waiting list of over fifty people. I don't know how God worked that out, but I am grateful that he did because of the great care I got.

Miracle 14:

Go to the Hospital now!

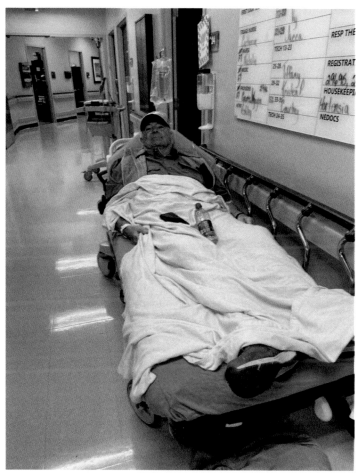

Bruce in ER Mansfield, TX experiencing kidney failure from an infection.

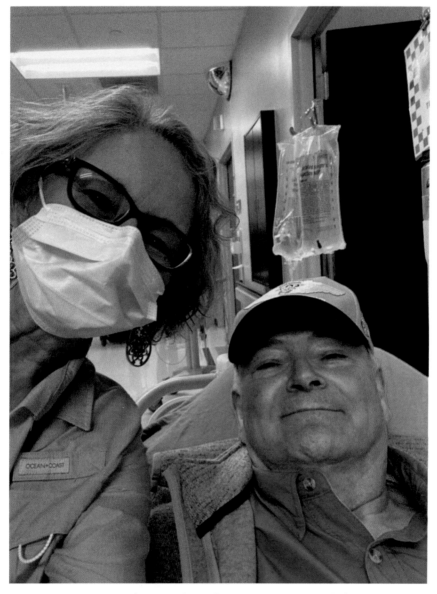

Bruce and Sister Kathryn Oliver in ER waiting treatment.

As a result of the many surgeries performed in Alaska to initially save my life, surgeons there opened an eleven-inch incision in my abdomen. For the incision to heal it was necessary to heal from the inside out with the aid of a wound vac. This is a machine that has a special seal put over the wound with tubes that run to and from it, which aids in the pumping of fluid in and out of the wound. I had this special machine attached to me the entire time I was in the hospital in Alaska. Changing the seal of this machine on my skin was a very painful process. It was changed every two to three days. Through this process, I learned the exercise of deep breathing and the "gutting-it-out" technique. No one said it was going to be easy!

Slowly, the wound began to heal, and by the time I was ready to leave Alaska, doctors felt a large patch over the remaining unhealed wound would suffice. This would allow the wound to continue to heal on its own without the continued aid of a wound vac. Several days before leaving the hospital, the wound vac was removed and a patch was applied. I am grateful for the good doctors in Alaska that got me to this point. The intent was to connect with a local doctor/nurse in Dallas that could continue to monitor the wound. Traveling with a wound vac would have been a big inconvenience. Thankfully, the doctors felt I was healed enough to travel without one.

Upon my arrival in Dallas, one of my sisters arranged for me to see a local doctor who specialized in wound care. Dr. Sykes was very talented at her specialty and started the process of nursing the remaining "holes" in me to health. When you have an incision as large as I had, the final section that ultimately closes up can take some time, which was the case for me. In addition to having a home health nurse come three times a week to change the bandage, I would visit Dr. Sykes weekly to have her monitor the healing progress. Ultimately, it ended up being a three-month process before the wound was fully healed.

During one of my weekly visits to Dr. Sykes, I noticed a concerned look on her face as she observed my wound. Apparently, she saw an infection that raised a red flag. She said she wanted me to immediately go to the Emergency Room! I remember saying, "Really, you think it is that bad?" I didn't feel any sicker than I had previously. She responded by saying, "I don't like what I am seeing; yes, go now!" Although I was shocked and surprised by her concern, I immediately went to the emergency room.

It took a while to get processed at the emergency room of the hospital in Mansfield, TX. Eventually they took me back to the treatment area and said they were so full I would need to lay on a bed out in the hall until a room opened up. My months of hospital care had sensitized me to being flexible and just rolling with whatever happened. As crazy as emergency rooms can be, it seemed especially abnormal when this was happening at 10:00 a.m. on a weekday. Ironically, I would be on the bed in the hall all day until 6:00 p.m. that night, when they moved me into a room in the ER.

The nurse came and immediately drew blood. Sometime later, the doctor came by and asked, "Have you ever had kidney failure?" I responded not that I was aware. He said, "Your numbers are off the charts!? We have had some problems with our testing lately; we will retake some blood and retest. Maybe it's our machine?!" They proceeded to repeat the testing process. Eventually, the doctor came back and confirmed my kidneys were off the chart and failing. They immediately hooked me up with an IV and proceeded to treat me. Eventually they admitted me to the hospital, and I was there for a period of time until they got the infection under control.

What a miracle that Dr. Sykes made the observant call for me to seek immediate medical care! I would have never guessed my condition was as severe as it ultimately ended up being. Thank you, God, for a caring doctor who acted on her instincts and pushed me to get the help I needed. This incident, along with many others, has only proved to me of God's continued care and watchful eye over my whole recovery process. How blessed I am that God has used another "angel" in the form of Dr. Sykes, to minister to my physical needs.

Miracle 15:

Encountering Jesus

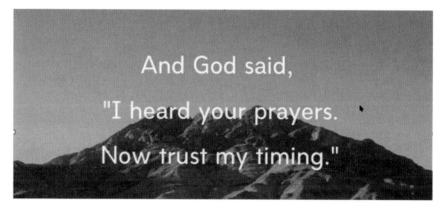

Trusting God's Timing

Coming out of the coma at Providence Hospital, I was hooked up to all kinds of tubes, IVs, a wound vac machine, and a boot on my broken ankle. I could move very little. All I could do was lay on my back in the hospital bed.

One night, in the middle of the night, I realized the only thing I could do was pray. It was quiet, except for the blurring sound of the medical equipment and the occasional beeps of the heart monitor. In the quietness of the night, I began praying. At first, I was talking to God, asking why this accident had happened. Why did I have to go through so much pain and suffering? I was basically having my own pity party. I kept praying, sometimes talking and asking questions of God, and sometimes just stopping to be quiet from the exhaustion of the praying.

At one point in the quietness, I had this vision of someone pulling two curtains apart, and I was transported to the foot of the cross on Golgotha Hill. My eyes were affixed to the body of Jesus. He was experiencing unbelievable pain. I saw the nails in His feet and hands. The tortured look on his face was a combination of the physical pain he felt and the weight of the sin he was bearing for the world. The anguish and pain were almost too much to look at. It was at that moment that I was overcome with sadness. It was the awareness that my sin had put Him on the cross. I started to cry, thinking of the unfairness! My sin was being put on the pure lamb of God! Oh, God, forgive me for my selfishness.

Oh, how insignificant my own physical pain was in relation to what I was witnessing with Jesus hanging there on the cross. With tears flowing down my cheeks and my heart broken in honor of Jesus, I couldn't help but be overcome with gratitude. I was so humbled by Jesus' gift of forgiveness and understanding. Jesus, if you went through that much pain on my behalf, certainly I can go through whatever pain I am currently experiencing! I was overwhelmed by His presence. Jesus, whatever you want me to do to honor you, I will do. When You give me opportunities to talk about You, I will do so. I saw the curtain close, and I knew I had experienced a peek into the Jesus I serve.

Miracle 16:

Insurance

Bruce riding the stationary bike in Physical Therapy

Toward the end of my hospital stay, there was a point at which the insurance company said they wanted to terminate my stay in the hospital. The staff came in one day and announced there was a possibility the insurance company was going to force me to leave within a matter of days. Panic set in because there were many issues still unresolved. Could I physically make it back to the lower forty-eight states to continue the rehabilitation? I still had a wound vac attached to me because a portion of the original eleven-inch incision was still open and not yet healed. What would I do about the open wound? Would I have to travel with a portable wound vac attached to my abdomen? How uncomfortable would that be?

The other major unanswered question was where I would be going to continue rehabilitation. There was a need for continued medical attention and lots of physical and nursing care. There were a number of options being considered, and just the thought of leaving the hospital prematurely was a big concern.

Leaving the hospital prematurely brought an overwhelming fear of the unknown, much like the momma bird kicking the little one out of the nest, and I wasn't ready to fly yet. It felt like an additional week was needed to physically and emotionally be ready to leave.

I asked Dr. MacNeil if there was any way she could help stall the process and get me another week or so to get healthier. Fortunately, she went to bat for me and was able to convince the insurance company to extend my stay another ten days. I felt such relief when I heard the news that extra time had been granted. I needed the miracle of additional time for my healing. Time was needed not just for physical healing, but I needed the time to prepare myself mentally and emotionally for the next phase of the recovery process. The gift of the extra time felt like a gift granted that was desperately needed.

In today's world, where insurance companies control so much of what happens in the medical field, it was truly a miracle that Dr. MacNeil was able to advocate on my behalf and secure the extra time. There was much to accomplish in the remaining time at the hospital, but at least I was granted a reprieve.

Miracle 17:

Faith that Sustains.

A group of Anchorage Motorcycle riders who took the time to pray for Bruce.

While in the coma, I was kept sedated with heavy drugs. It is a known fact that these drugs can produce wild dreams. I was no exception. There were numerous crazy dreams I had. I dreamed the owners of Providence Hospital were part of the drug cartel and kept me sedated to keep me quiet! I also believed I was being sequestered on the hospital's private yacht that was crossing the US, stopping in towns like Celina, OH, Fort Wayne, IN, and Hinsdale, IL. The truth is, Providence is the largest private employer in the State of Alaska, with over 4,000 employees. Yes, I had to smile and laugh when I would later recognize the absurdity of the dreams.

I did have one dream in particular that was as real as if I were there physically. In the dream, I was lying in bed. The room was pitch black, and darkness was everywhere. I felt the darkness, both physically and spiritually. There was an overwhelming feeling of helplessness. I was crying and wanting God to help me out of this dark place. All of a sudden, out of the darkness, I heard the voice of my pastor, Jeff Linthicum. I couldn't make out what he said, but just hearing his voice gave me hope in the darkness. I then heard the voice of Chris talking about the playing of her French horn at church. I could also hear the voice of my cousin, Darlene Nelson. Both of these gave me more hope. Then I felt the physical presence of Brandon and Jessica Hill, friends from Berne, IN, standing just to the left of me. Their presence represented care and concern.

While still in the coma, something spectacular happened. If one has ever been in a concert where the lights are turned down and people turn their cell phone lights on and start to waive them in the air, that is exactly what happened. The darkness of the room was being illuminated by all the cell phone lights coming on. I simultaneously realized that every one of those lights represented someone who was praying for me. My heart started to fill with gratitude to God for showing up and bringing light into my life. The tears flowed. In a moment that felt like good and evil were wrestling for my life, God showed up and said, "He is mine!" I knew that His light shines in the darkness, and the darkness cannot penetrate it. I felt peace and calm because I knew that God would win, and that he was there for me. Was it a dream? Yes, but it was a dream that had God directing it at a very critical time in my physical survival.

As I came out of the coma and started to get a sense of still being alive, I experienced an interesting realization. When scripture verses were hard to remember, the one thing I could do was pray. I have always found it hard to memorize scripture verses. I think that is why God has had to keep my nose in His word on a daily basis.

As I experienced pain, discomfort, and the realization of the seriousness of my physical condition, I found the one thing I was able to do was pray. I would close my eyes and bury my thoughts about getting to know Jesus. I could only minimally identify with the pain He went through while hanging on the cross. Yes, I was in lots of pain, but I was weeping tears as I realized the pain and agony he went through on the cross just for me. How could I complain about the pain I was going through when His pain far outpaced mine.

There was such peace and comfort as I heard him whispering, "I'm with you!" Many times, often in the quiet of the night, I would mentally, emotionally, and spiritually go to meet Jesus and just be in His presence. There was such peace and understanding when I felt like I was transformed in His presence. I knew I could trust Him. I could trust His mercies to touch my life. I felt like He had rescued me and given me a new purpose—to talk about Him. It is only because of Him that I am here today. Why would I not want to give Him the glory and praise for intervening and saving my life?! Thank you, Jesus.

Miracle 18:

Where to go for Rehab?

Gerald and Kathryn Oliver, Brother-in-law and sister in Dallas, TX area.)

Bruce, David Oliver, and Gerald Oliver at Car/Airshow, Dallas, TX

Where do I go after leaving the hospital in Alaska?! This involved a week of hard decision-making, both logistically and emotionally. I needed a place where I could continue getting medical care as well as physical therapy. The choices were the farm in Ohio, Chicago, and Dallas. It was a week of my family exploring lots of options in all locations.

What finally became apparent was an assisted living facility in Midlothian, Texas, where I could get medical assistance and physical therapy. They had an opening, and I was able to fly directly from Anchorage to Dallas and be situated in the facility all on the same day. My sister, Kathy Oliver, and her husband, Gerald, live in Midlothian. While Gerald was flying to Texas with me, Kathy had furniture and necessary items moved to the assisted living facility. Both Kathy and Gerald wanted to have me come so they could help take care of me. God clearly opened the right doors, at the right time, and in the right location.

I was able to receive home health, which meant nursing and physical therapy coming to the facility. Midlothian, Texas, was also where, several years earlier, I had a local surgeon remove part of my colon because of a growth. Four months later, I would be able to use the same surgeon to reverse the ostomy bag by surgically re-hooking up my internal plumbing. Because of the good health care in the Dallas area, I was able to connect with eight various doctors that aided in my recovery. The fact that I was able to get the medical attention I needed in such a short time is truly a miracle.

Miracle 19:

CREF (Commercial Real Estate Fellowship) Breakfast

Bruce speaking at Chicago Commercial Real Estate Fellowship Breakfast, December 2023

Bruce's first visit back to the office with a warm reception.

On December 7th, 2023, I was invited to share my story of faith, specifically my recent Alaska motorcycle accident, in Chicago at the CREF (Commercial Real Estate Fellowship) breakfast. This event is held annually at the Hyatt O'Hare Regency, with well over 700 people in attendance. The purpose of the breakfast is to bring real estate professionals and friends together to celebrate Christmas and the birth of Jesus. The format is for a local real estate person to share their faith journey, and then there is a guest speaker to follow.

In September 2023, John Picchiotti from the CREF committee called me and asked if I would be willing and able to share my testimony. I immediately said yes.

From the early days in the hospital in Anchorage, I told God I would be willing to share my story of survival with anyone. I already knew in my heart that the committee was going to ask me to share, long before John called me. I knew that God wanted His story of faith working through me to be told. As much as it is an honor to speak at the breakfast, I felt God inspiring me to share His story, His goodness, and His power of restoration.

At the time I agreed to speak, I was still facing some health issues but felt confident I would be ready to travel by the December date.

I flew to Chicago on December 6th, the day before the breakfast, and had dinner that night with some special friends I had invited to join me. These were friends that were instrumental in my Alaska recovery in one way or another. These friends included, Floyd and Arlene Hoffman, Mike and Marsha Bear, Bryan and Lynne Barus, Hank and Gail Amabile, and Tim and Nancy Bailey. We had a wonderful dinner together, and I was blessed by their presence, their friendship, and their support. They were present for the breakfast the following morning.

The breakfast on Thursday, December 7th, was the first time I had seen any of my business colleagues from Chicago since my accident. My company, NAI Hiffman, had over fifty people there. I had invited thirty guests. Friends from several Bible study groups came as well. It felt so nice to be back among friends and business associates.

After the meal, I was the first speaker on the agenda. I had worked many hours on my talk and had a dozen or so photos that were flashed up on the big screens as I talked. The pictures illustrated me laying in the middle of the road with the paramedics around me. There was a picture of the life-jet that transported me from Fairbanks to Anchorage, paramedics transporting me between hospitals, and a picture of my helmet. My full-faced helmet showed the deep gouges the rough Alaska Highway took out of it, clearly sparing my face and life!

As I told the story of the accident, I also interspersed my faith journey as a believer in Jesus. I could feel the presence of God's Holy Spirit not only guiding me in my delivery but also reaching the hearts of the listeners. I remember at one point in the talk between sentences, I paused briefly and was aware it was deathly silent in the room. God was using the words and message to reach the listeners. At the conclusion of the talk, I was surprised by a standing ovation. My heart was warmed. I was more moved by God's power to use His story through me to touch others. I received so many uplifting comments, emails, and phone calls from people in attendance.

Fortunately, a friend of mine recorded the talk with his iPhone and later sent me a YouTube link that I have been able to share with many people who were not in attendance. I know God has used that simple recording to further the reach of His story. Again, God knows just how to orchestrate His message. To Him be all the glory.

There were many comments made, like, "I can't believe how well you look given what you have been through!" The miracle of being able to stand and deliver a speech within six months of all the trauma of the accident was amazing, even to me.

Following the breakfast, I was able to go to the office at NAI Hiffman and greet many of my colleagues that I had not seen in six months. They had a luncheon reception to welcome me back. It was very nice.

Miracle 20:

From coma to walking out of the hospital.

Bruce with sisters Carolyn Fitzsimons and Kathryn Oliver

Mucho Lake, BC Canada

The hospital stay in Alaska stretched for seventy-two days. Initially, I was in intensive care and recovery at Providence Hospital in Anchorage. After a period of recovery, it was decision time as to where to go for the next phase of rehabilitation and recovery. While there was lots of anguish and investigation of options by my family, the answer to many prayers came at a place called St. Elias Specialty Rehabilitation Hospital there in Anchorage. This hospital was part of the Providence Hospital network, but it was not a given that I would qualify. Fortunately, by the grace of God, I was selected as a qualified candidate and was eventually admitted. Later, I would find out that there was a waiting list of over fifty people waiting to get into the hospital. That one, I cannot explain.

This specialty hospital had two floors and a limited number of beds. I spent a period of time on the first floor continuing to recover from my wounds. During this period, they would use Hoyer lifts to get me out of bed, into a wheelchair, and outside to smell the freshness of the Alaska summers.

One day the nurse wheeled me over to the window to see a moose walking through the bushes outside the hospital. Only in Alaska!!

At a certain point, they said I was qualified to be moved to the second floor of the hospital for the rehabilitation portion of the hospital. They said I would be doing close to 6 hours a day of rehabilitation activity, and I would be expected to work hard. I will be honest and tell you I was scared! I am not one to be afraid of hard work. What scared me was knowing the expectations of "moving" and "gaining control of my body" when I was still bed-fast and barely able to sit up in bed without falling over. I responded and said, "Bring it on, I will give it everything I have."

As a farm boy, I was fortunate to grow up learning the value of hard work. If there was one quality I learned from my father, it was to not shy away from work and be willing to give it your all. The rehabilitation was "brutal!" From the time they transported me in my bed up to the second floor of the hospital to start rehabilitation, they were pushing me to "move!" Every morning at about 5:00 a.m. I would get a schedule delivered to my room outlining the activities for the day. Usually, the sessions would be anywhere from forty-five minutes to a couple hours. The sessions were exhausting, whether it was relearning how to walk, climb stairs, button my shirt, pedal the bike, make a grilled cheese sandwich, or even try to take a shower. Sometimes there would be a forty-five -minute break between sessions, and it was all I could do to crawl back into bed and collapse. Eventually all this hard work paid off, and there were discussions of kicking me out of the rehab hospital and making plans for me to make it back to the "lower forty-eight states" as the saying goes. The process of going from being in a coma and fighting for my life to being able to walk out of the hospital in seventy-two days is nothing short of a miracle.

Miracle 21:

Lessons Learned

Lessons learned from my Alaska experience.

1. Look for the positive and God in every moment.

2. To have friends, you have to be a friend.

3. We never know how God wants to use us to touch people's lives.

4. The hard lessons we have to learn help mold our character if we are willing to see God working through the pain.

5. Our plans are secondary to His plans.

6. Look for the angels because they are all around.

7. The power of prayer changes things. Maybe most importantly, it changes me.

8. Don't be afraid to be honest with God and tell him the desires of your heart.

9. God's timing is always right.

10. Trust him in the good times and the bad times.

11. Look beyond your own pain and see the goodness of those around you.

12. When you have prayed and laid everything at his feet, trust him that whatever the results are, it will be okay.

13. Even in pain, learn to love others.

14. Look for the miracles God does every day.

15. Know that God uses open and closed doors to guide us.

16. Be willing to look for and listen to the stories of others. Everybody has a story.

17. Whatever your gift, God will use it.

18. Cultivate a lifestyle of gratefulness.

19. When God's Holy Spirit speaks to your heart, be willing to act on it.

20. God wins over darkness.

Mucho Lake BC Canada

Meziadin Lake, BC Canada

Welcome to Alaska

Mountains at Mucho Lake BC Canada

Water and Mountains at Mucho Lake, BC Canada

Bruce at the Arctic Ocean